In Defense of the Accidental

Philosophical Studies

ODO MARQUARD

Translated by Robert M. Wallace

D0171252

New York   Oxford
OXFORD UNIVERSITY PRESS
1991

Oxford University Press

Oxford   New York   Toronto
Delhi   Bombay   Calcutta   Madras   Karachi
Petaling Jaya   Singapore   Hong Kong   Tokyo
Nairobi   Dar es Salaam   Cape Town
Melbourne   Auckland

and associated companies in
Berlin   Ibaden

Copyright © 1991 by Oxford University Press, Inc.

Published by Oxford University Press, Inc.,
200 Madison Avenue, New York, New York 10016

Original title of German edition:
Apologie des Zufälligen

Oxford is a registered trademark of Oxford University Press

All rights reserved. No part of this publication may be reproduced,
stored in a retrieval system, or transmitted, in any form or by any means,
electronic, mechanical, photocopying, recording, or otherwise,
without the prior permission of Oxford University Press.

Library of Congress Cataloging-in-Publication Data
Marquard, Odo.
[Apologie des Zufälligen. English]
In defense of the accidental : philosophical studies /
Odo Marquard ; translated by Robert M. Wallace.
p.   cm.   — (Odeon)
Translation of: Apologie des Zufälligen.
Includes bibliographical references and index.
ISBN 0-19-505632-9
ISBN 0-19-507252-9 (pbk.)
1. Philosophy.   2. Culture—Philosophy.   I. Title.
B29.M36774513   1991
193—dc20   90-41998   CIP

2 4 6 8 9 7 5 3 1

Printed in the United States of America
on acid-free paper

IN DEFENSE OF
THE ACCIDENTAL

ODÉON

JOSUÉ V. HARARI AND VINCENT DESCOMBES
General Editors

HERMENEUTICS AS POLITICS
Stanley Rosen

FAREWELL TO MATTERS OF PRINCIPLE
Philosophical Studies
Odo Marquard

THE LACANIAN DELUSION
François Roustang

A THEATER OF ENVY
William Shakespeare
René Girard

IN DEFENSE OF THE ACCIDENTAL
Philosophical Studies
Odo Marquard

LIBRARY
ALMA COLLEGE
ALMA, MICHIGAN

Contents

LIBRARY
KENT COLLEGE
[ILLEGIBLE], MICHIGAN

Author's Note

This little volume is a collection of seven essays written for various occasions between 1982 and 1986. All of them—without any particular order—advocate the same position, which is the philosophy of a skeptic and "usualist" who derives from, and has never entirely escaped, the hermeneutic school. Consequently all of them aim—directly or indirectly, and with the brevity of human life as their argument—at the thesis that what we human beings are is always more our accidents than our choice. Beyond that, almost all of these essays have a special relationship to the Berlin *Wissenschaftskolleg* [Institute for Advanced Study], of which I was a fellow during its second year. Almost all were either completed or begun there. Here, as in other areas, I have much to be grateful for: "Wenn ich bedenke, wie man wenig ist, / und was man ist, das blieb man andern schuldig" [When I consider how little one is— and what one is, one owes to other people] (Goethe, *Torquato Tasso,* lines 105–6).

IN DEFENSE OF
THE ACCIDENTAL

=== 1 ===

Skeptics: A Speech of Thanks

Respected Dignitaries!
Ladies and Gentlemen!

First of all I have, by inclination, the duty to thank the German Academy for Language and Poetry for conferring on me the 1984 Sigmund Freud Prize for Scholarly Writing, which I have done little—in fact, very little—to deserve, so that my receiving it is a happy accident. What we human beings are is always more our accidents than our accomplishments. Thanks are one form of that which, for this reason, is always unavoidable for us: acquiescence in the accidental.

In return—*en revanche,* as they say—I will offer some observations about skeptics, of whom I am one. In other words, I will show my colors, which are camouflage colors. I am, as a professional, what I would have been as an amateur: I am a philosopher. It is true that not only does the philosopher give the world some nuts, that is, riddles, to crack, but the world gives them to the philosopher as well. It does not follow from this that the philosopher is a nutcracker [*Nussknacker*]; for—*in nuce*—what he deals with is not nuts but the mind, the *nous:* Philosophers are *nous*-crackers. At any rate, that is true of the kind of philosopher of which it is least certain whether this kind really counts as philosophers. I mean, precisely, the skeptics.

Sextus Empiricus divided philosophers into those who thought that they had found (dogmatists), those who maintained that one cannot find (academic skeptics), and those who are still seeking (Pyrrhonian skeptics). Thus there are two factions among skeptics, and one can wind up in the wrong faction: among the advocates—compulsively and incessantly doubting everything—of academic skepticism. When one has dispatched this faction by argument, there still remains the other and much more tenacious faction, which, for example, experiences an occasional refutation of its position as a refreshing shot in the arm; because it understands skepticism as the virtuous mean between two vices: absolute knowledge and absolute ignorance. It is this faction that I speak of here: of the Pyrrhonian skeptics, and consequently, of course, also of the moralists, and large parts of the delayed moralistic writings of the delayed nation:[a] that is, of historicism,[b] and the skeptics of the hermeneutic school. Their skepticism has, I think, three distinctive characteristics.

First, skepticism is an appreciation of the separation of powers. Skeptical doubt—as the word *Zweifel* [doubt] (which in its *zwei* [two] also contains multiplicity) betrays—is the procedure (known in the school as "isosthenes diaphonia") of letting two opposed convictions collide with each other. This collision causes both convictions to decline so much in power that the individual—*divide et fuge!* [divide and escape!]—as the laughing or crying third party, gets free of them, gaining distance and his or her own distinct individuality. There need not be only two convictions; several convictions can also hold each other in check. And not only convictions, but also completely different reciprocally balancing, compensating magnitudes in reality can achieve this liberating effect. For doubt is a special case of the separation of powers, which has a general importance for the skeptic, as the separation of every "sole" power into plural powers—of history into histories or stories, of social and economic power into social and economic powers, of philosophy into philosophies, and so forth. Montesquieu's doctrine of the political "separation of powers," which stands in the tradition of skeptical moralism, illuminates only one special region of this phenomenon, by which the skeptic sets great store in general: the liberating effect of the overall, power-separating motleyness of the reality we live in.

Second, skepticism is "usualism," an appreciation of the usual, and of the unavoidability of usual practices. As skepticism insists, we do not live long enough to arrive at absolute orientations—at the absolutely correct management of the absolutely correct life, which depends on finding absolute truth. Our death always comes more quickly than this absolute orientation. That is why we inevitably remain predominantly (and I emphasize not *only,* but predominantly) what we already were: We remain our past, of which the usual—what is accepted because it was accepted in the past—is part. Our life is too short to escape as far as we might like to from what is usual—from the existing mores, customs, traditions—into the absolute, or wherever else. Skepticism becomes moralism by taking account of this unavoidability of customary modes of behavior, of mores: Great leaps, and (still more) absolute ones, are not human.

Third, skepticism is, for that very reason, a willingness to accept one's own contingency. This has nothing to do with taking pleasure in arbitrariness. The concept of the contingent, the accidental, of the finite, which originated in the Christian theology of creation, does define it as "that which could also be different." But if one looks at it not from God's point of view but, more humanly, from man's point of view, this accidentalness takes two forms. The accidental is that which could also be different and which could be changed by us (for example, this talk, which I could give in one way or in a different way); in other words, it is something arbitrarily accidental. Or the accidental is that which could also be different and which we precisely cannot change, or can change only a little (because it is a stroke of fate, which resists negation—such as, for example, having been born); in other words, it is something fatefully accidental. Now the skeptic thinks that in our lives the fateful accidents leave an indelible imprint; and among them are also our usual practices, on which we have to rely, because we do not, predominantly, govern our lives ourselves, and certainly do not do so absolutely. But this means that what we human beings are is always more our accidents—our fateful accidents—than our accomplishments. I do not say that we are *only* our accidents. All I say is that we are not only our accomplishments, but also our accidents—our fateful accidents. To which I make only one additional qualification:

We are always more our accidents than our accomplishments. So we have to be able to bear what is accidental, because living with what is accidental is not a result of failing to reach the absolute, but is our historically normal condition.

The fateful accidents in my own life are not limited to the fact that I exist and that I exist right here, where a friendly academy is conferring Sigmund Freud Prizes for Scholarly Writing. Nor are my fateful accidents limited to the fact that I came to philosophy immediately after the war, and that no doubt for that reason—through a perennialization of my alarm, and through my conversion of a perplexed state of mind into a philosophical position—I arrived, specifically, at skepticism. An additional fateful accident was this: At some early point during my university studies I accidentally encountered, in my aunt's bookcase, Freud's *Introductory Lectures on Psychoanalysis;* this discovery happened to occur during the semester in which my teacher of philosophy, Joachim Ritter, gained my allegiance (as it turned out, a pretty much lifelong allegiance) to his way of thinking, through his lectures on aesthetics. I was amazed, then, by the similarity between certain fundamental patterns in the psychoanalytic theory and in his philosophy—which, however, derived, in the broadest sense, from German Idealism—and I asked myself: Why should that be the case? To answer this question, I wrote my *Habilitationsschrift* (at a time when Freud was as yet hardly a topic for discussion among philosophers here in Germany) on psychoanalysis as a form taken by German Idealism—a treatise that a friendly accident then protected from being published.[c] Thus I am indebted (and this is the only reason why I mention this here) to a greater than average extent to the patron-by-name of the prize that is being conferred on me—to Sigmund Freud. I am, however, indebted not as a patient of his students (life already seemed difficult enough to me without that), but certainly as a theoretician and a practitioner of transcendental belles-lettres. That was a life-guiding accident that I neither can nor want to change, but in which I acquiesce.

There are various forms of acquiescence in the accidental. The "extreme reactions" of laughing and crying are among these, as is the extreme reaction that is reason: the abandonment of the effort to remain stupid. Thanks, as I said in the beginning, are also a way of acquiescing in the accidental, and that also includes (as I wanted to underline, by complying with the customary practice of giving a speech of thanks here) acquiescence in the happy accident that this prize represents for me. I thank you.

Translator's Notes

a. "The delayed nation," *die verspätete Nation,* alludes to a book published by Helmuth Plessner in Zurich in 1935 and reissued under this title in 1959 (Stuttgart). The "laughing or crying third party," in the next paragraph (which alludes to another of Plessner's works, *Lachen und Weinen* [2nd ed., Bern, 1950]; *Laughing and Crying,* trans. J. Churchill and M. Grene [Evanston, 1970]), is explained in the final paragraph of the last chapter in this collection: "In Defense of the Accidental."

b. Like the majority of writers in German, the author uses *Historismus,* "historicism," to refer to the modern appreciation of historical individuality—of epochs, cultures, events—and of processes of development (the sense analyzed and chronicled by F. Meinecke in his *Die Entstehung des Historismus* [Munich and Berlin, 1936]), rather than to the fascination with historical "wholes" and their (possibly predictive) "laws," which Sir Karl Popper referred to as "historicism" in his polemical works.

c. This thesis, whose acceptance by the University of Münster qualified the author as a university lecturer, was entitled *Über die Depotenzierung der Transzendentalphilosophie. Einige philosophische Motive eines neueren Psychologismus in der Philosophie* (1963). It has in fact finally been published, under the altered title, *Transzendentaler Idealismus, romantische Naturphilosophie, Psychoanalyse* (Cologne, 1986).

2

Unburdenings: Theodicy Motives
in Modern Philosophy

Today there is a prevailing, widespread tendency to require everything and everyone to legitimate itself or herself or himself. Everything is supposed to enter a "context of justification" (of which the luxury model is the so-called "dominance-free discourse") and to justify itself, especially if it has entered a legitimation crisis—and today, in what people like to call the "postconventional" age, that seems to be the case with everything. And if a legitimation crisis should still be absent anywhere, it is, if need be, invented—in the interest of making the demand for justification ubiquitous. For today everything seems to need justification: the family, the state, causality, the individual, chemistry, vegetables, the way one's hair grows, one's mood, one's life, education, bathing suits; only one thing—one wonders why—needs no justification, and that is the need to justify to one and all. If, in an effort to be polite, I introduce myself: "Allow me: My name is Marquard," it seems that the normal answer nowadays has to be: "Nothing is allowed here until it is justified! By what right are you Marquard in the way that you are, and not in an entirely different way? And by what right are you at all, rather than not being?" This boom in the demand for justification is a phenomenon that needs to be seen, and which therefore needs a name. Because it makes everything into, as it were, a tribunal, I call it the "tribunalization" of the reality of modern life.

This boom in the demand for justification is not something that just appeared on the scene. When each thing and each person has the total burden of proof for its right to exist and its right to be as it is, one is tempted to say that the expectation that one will bear this burden, which far exceeds any quota, in former times, of "good works," is— like capitalism (freely adapting Max Weber) or (freely adapting myself) the modern apotheosis of aesthetically good works, or of works of art—the revenge, against its proscription, of the "justification by works" that the Reformation proscribed. This revenge now takes the form of the pressure (unrelieved by divine grace) for total justification. This was initially, if I see it correctly, the pattern of the tribunal mania of the French Revolution, and of its practice, beginning in 1793, of treating everyone as "suspect" until he or she had proved to be the opposite. But according to the view taken by Hegel and his school, German Idealism was a parallel action to the French Revolution: "Our German philosophy," Heine wrote in 1835, was the "dream of the French Revolution." "As in France every privilege, so in Germany every thought had to justify itself"; "our philosophical Jacobins gathered around the *Critique of Pure Reason*. . . . Kant was our Robespierre."[1] Kant's first Critique was the initiating work of transcendental revolutionary Idealism, which Fichte's *Science of Knowledge* radicalized. In a "legal action before "reason's court of justice," the a prioris—which are suspected, gnoseologically and historically, of bad character—are supposed to justify themselves (and thereby the human "I"),[2] and only then receive their "certificat du civisme" as citizens in the realm of science and history. Can man's good character in regard to science and history be vindicated? "Si scientia, unde metaphysica? Si progressus, unde repressio?" [If there is science, why is there metaphysics? If there is progress, why is there repression?] Just as, concretely, revolutionary Jacobinism tribunalized political reality, so transcendentally revolutionary Idealism—with these questions—tribunalizes philosophy into a proceeding of man versus man in matters relating to scientific and historical evil, so that, like its intensification in Marx and Nietzsche and its "ultimatist" and pragmatic variants in Habermas and Apel, it is part of the history of the tribunalization of the reality in which we, as modern people, live.

Now in my opinion this proceeding, with its curriculum of accusation and justification, is prefigured in Leibniz's *Theodicy*. This work is, in modern times, the initial philosophical (and I emphasize *philosophical*) tribunal. It was Leibniz's *Theodicy* that first—three quarters of a century before Kant's *Critique* and Fichte's *Science of Knowledge*—made philosophy, in its central role, into a tribunal: into the proceeding of man versus God in matters relating to the evils in the world. Leibnizian theodicy and transcendentally revolutionary Idealism agree in their fundamental procedural nature. Both are a proceeding, a tribunal, with evils as the subject of the accusation and with a corresponding task of vindication, in connection with which man is the accuser and the defender. From this I conclude that both of them—Leibniz's theodicy and Kant's and Fichte's transcendentally revolutionary Idealism—are part of the phenomenon of the tribunalization of the reality of modern life, and that the philosophical beginning of this tribunalization, which still fundamentally dominates (indeed, especially dominates) the present, is in Leibniz's *Theodicy*. Putting it differently, and as a thesis, I suggest that this tribunalization is a theodicy motive in modern philosophy.

There are several such theodicy motives in modern philosophy. In addition to the one that I have already mentioned—tribunalization—I would like to point out three others here. Admittedly, the motives in question are ones that attempt, precisely, to ward off the burden represented by tribunalization—that is, they are "unburdening" motives. "Unburdening" [*Entlastung*] is not only a term that was successfully introduced into anthropology by Arnold Gehlen,[a] but is also a concept in the law of associations and in criminal law: Boards of directors, suspects, human beings and gods can be "unburdened" [in English: have their reports approved, or be exonerated]—or not, as the case may be. Of course, one cannot discuss theodicy motives like these without mentioning theodicy. So my remaining discussion falls into four, rather than three, parts, as follows: theodicy and the modern age; the theodicy motive of autonomization; the theodicy motive of bettering the bad; and the theodicy motive of compensation.

Theodicy and the Modern Age

"By 'theodicy,' we understand the defense of the highest wisdom of the Author of the world against the charges that reason brings against it on account of the aspects of the world which are not in harmony with its purpose." This is how Kant in 1791,[3] looking back on the failure of the optimistic theodicy, defines the undertaking—theodicy, as a specifically modern philosophy—that Leibniz, the term's inventor, launched as a philosophical discipline with his *Essais de Théodicée sur la bonté de Dieu, la liberté de l'homme et l'origine du mal,* published in 1710. It is true that the question about God's righteous goodness, in view of the evils in the world that he created, seems to be a very old one. It was, it seems, already raised in the Book of Job; and the formula, "Si Deus, unde malum?" [If God exists, why is there evil?] is after all already found in Lactantius's *De ira dei* [On the wrath of God], where it is in turn presented as a question posed by Epicurus.[4] Nevertheless, I maintain—encouraged by my opinion that theodicy's question was always blunted in earlier, premodern times, by an intact religion—that theodicy is specifically modern: Where there is theodicy, there is modernity, and where there is modernity, there is theodicy. Allow me to make two remarks that may give this proposition something approaching plausibility.

My first remark is the following: the modern age was the first one in which theodicy became *possible,* because the modern age was the first one that had the necessary distance, in relation to evils—the *malum metaphysicum,* finitude, the *malum morale,* evil, the *malum physicum,* suffering, and perhaps other *mala* as well. Experience of life seems to me to show that when one is up against suffering, under its immediate pressure, the problem is never theodicy; for what is important then is simply the ability to hold up through one's suffering or one's sympathy. It is stamina in enduring, in helping, and in comforting. How can I reach the next year, the next day, the next hour? In the face of this question, theodicy is not an issue, because a mouthful of bread, a breathing space, a slight alleviation, a moment of sleep are all more important in these circumstances than the accusation and the defense of God. Only when the direct pressure of suffering and compassion relents, under conditions of distance, do we arrive at theodicy. So this occurs, representatively, in the modern age. For the modern age is the age of distance: the first epoch in which impotence and suffering are not the taken-for-granted and normal state of affairs for human beings. Now, for the first time, want seems, in principle, masterable; pain avoidable; sickness conquerable; wickedness abolishable; and man's (finitude-induced) impotence outmaneuverable. Because evils cease to be matters of course, it seems that one needs God less and less as the Redeemer, so that henceforth—in the modern age, the age of distance—one can call him properly to account as the Creator, through theodicy. That does not prevent the discussion from being vehement, for the rule here is that of the increasing intensity of remainders: The more negative things are abolished, the more vexatious—precisely as they diminish—the negative things that remain become. But the fundamental principle is that the task of theodicy becomes possible (and then also real, and central) under conditions of distance; and thus it is representatively so in the age of distance, the modern age.

My second remark is this one: The modern age was the first one in which theodicy became *necessary,* and this is because theodicy denies talk of an evil creator god. It is thus an answer (as Leibniz's references show) to a position that really did speak of an evil creator god: a position that was (in the context of Gnosticism and Manichaeism) above all the position of Marcion, who, being impressed by the delay of the Parousia, believed that the only way for humans to be saved from the evil world was by an entirely different, unworldly redeemer god, a god who, battling with the world's evil creator, destroys it in a redeeming eschatology. As a world-conserving age, the modern age opposes this: It is (as Hans Blumenberg says) an "overcoming" of Gnosticism, the "second" overcoming, in fact, because the first one— the Middle Ages—proved unsuccessful.[5] The first, medieval refutation of Marcion was the discovery of human freedom by Origen and Augustine, by which (as God's alibi) all the world's evils are imputed, morally, to man, as his sin, so that the principle that "omne ens est bonum" [all being is good] can continue to hold in respect of God. This first refutation of Marcion is finally retracted by nominalism's

intensification of the theology of omnipotence and by Luther's doctrine of the *servum arbitrium* [subject will]. In this way, the creator god
is again burdened with the world's evils. He evades this burden, in the
role of the alien and hidden redeemer God who at the same time no
longer orders anything intelligibly in the world, so that human beings
have to dispute—ultimately in a bloody manner—about questions of
salvation. The religious civil wars make manifest the terrifying side of
the world's end that is supposed to end in salvation; here delivery from
evils presents itself as itself an evil, which—as, for example, the reason
for permanent civil war—has to be put out of operation: The eschatology of redemption has to be neutralized. This neutralization of the
eschatology of redemption is the modern age. For if the modern age is
to be possible, the urgency of redemption must be removed by an
attempted demonstration that this world is endurable, even in the
absence of the saving end, thanks to many a "rose in the cross of the
present"[b]; in other words, its creator was not a wicked god, and the
world is not an evil world. This attempted demonstration, the second
refutation of Marcion, is theodicy. It became necessary and remained
necessary for the foundation of the modern age. Hence the validity of
what I said earlier—that theodicy belongs specifically to the modern
age.

These two remarks were meant to alleviate the strangeness of my
thesis that where there is theodicy, there is modernity, and where there
is modernity, there is theodicy. Now because the modern age, even
today, has still not come to an end (which, as a traditionalist of modernity, I regard as fortunate), that also means that theodicy survives the
crisis of its life-form that sets in around 1750: The "system" of optimism is outlived, in the modern period, by at least "motives" of
theodicy. Here there are a number of strategies for survival: for example, the old solution (or parts of it) uncouples itself from the problem
of theodicy (which it cannot solve satisfactorily) and adopts new problems, whose satisfactory solution it becomes; or else the question of
theodicy survives its old answer and looks for a new answer, ultimately at the cost of its original intention. I will now discuss the
second case first.

The Theodicy Motive of Autonomization

Leibniz, in his *Theodicy,* defends God as the best possible Creator of the best possible world, providing a reassuringly sober argument for his system of optimism: God is not wicked, but neither is he a merely "principled" Creator [*Gesinnungsschöpfer*]ᶜ who—in an unworldly way, disregarding detrimental side effects—only *means* well; rather, he is a worldly-wise "responsible" Creator who endeavors, paying heed to compossibilities, to "make the best of it." On the basis of an optimizing calculation that is aware of marginal utility (the kind of calculation that might come naturally to a thinker in the age of mercantilism), God permits those evils in the world that—as *conditiones sine quibus non* [necessary conditions]—increase the overall goodness of his creation, making it not, indeed, the "good" world, but the "best possible" world, at any rate. Creation is the art of the best possible.

This Leibnizian solution to the problem of unburdening God leaves at least one question unanswered: If the best possible creation is only the best possible, and inevitably includes evils, why then did God not refrain from creating it? Especially since one of God's traditional alibis, the devil, had been derealized by Descartes not long before into the *genius malignus* [wicked demon], as a trick of argumentation in the context of "methodical doubt," and had thus ceased to be available as a means of unburdening God, this question of the grounds for the Creation as such was made urgent, in the middle of the eighteenth century, by striking new experiences of "badness": for instance, the proto-"Green" negative experience of the remoteness of culture from nature, which Rousseau described, beginning in 1750; and, for another instance, Kant's discovery (beginning in 1769) of the antinomies, with the alarming consequence that the guarantor of the Enlightenment—reason—can itself operate as a *genius malignus,* through its own endogenously generated illusions. This new discomfort with the world—for which the earthquake of Lisbon served as a visible focus, and to which the almost simultaneous beginning of the literary and historiographical fear genres, the genre of the horror novel (1764) and the genre of the philosophy of history (1765), also belong—now ruins optimism and calls for a radical answer to our question: If the best possible creation inevitably includes evils, why did God not refrain from creating it? A radical answer to this question is provided by the philosophy of autonomy, beginning with Kant and Fichte, and this answer is: God *did* refrain from creating it, for it is not God who creates the world, but—in accordance with the principle of autonomy—man, who does so specifically (according to Kant) as the creator of the artificial experimental world of the exact sciences, and the world of their technical application, as well as the world of autonomously self-given moral norms and their fulfillment; and (according to Fichte) as the creator of history. I underscore the fact that this uncommonly influential thesis—the autonomy thesis, beginning with transcendentally revolutionary idealism—was made necessary by theodicy, as a way of unburdening God by relieving him of his duties as the Creator god, whose successor (with the job of unburdening God) is man the autonomous creator. So my thesis[6] is: This autonomization—a sort of atheism *ad maiorem Dei gloriam* [to the greater glory of God] (a phenomenon to which, accordingly, the doctrine and later the myth of the "end of God" also belong)—this autonomization is a theodicy motive in modern philosophy.

Thus in theodicy the position of the one who is accused—a position that God, for reasons of theodicy, vacates—now comes to be occupied by man. I may remind the reader of what I said at the beginning about "tribunalization": Now man is the accused party before this tribunal. He escapes this tribunal only by becoming it: Nominating himself to the role of the Redeemer-man (who, with a monopoly on accusation, is the avant-garde and represents only the future), he brings a case—in matters of evil in the world—against the other human beings, as obstructors of emancipation, as wicked Creator-men,[d] and condemns them forthwith to becoming the past, through revolution. What we find in this revolution in the name of autonomy and of the philosophy of history—in the French Revolution, in the first place—is that when the good Redeemer-men rule, instead of the wicked Creator-men, the evils do not disappear, but remain and expand. If mankind is not to be disheartened by this disappointment of the revolutionary "immediate expectation," one must finally—so as to articulate the experience of powerlessness, and to find a scapegoat—reactivate God as the creator of the adverse circumstances. Of course this philosophical recall of

God, which occurs (representatively) beginning in 1800, renews the task of theodicy, in the literal sense, but this time in the context of the philosophy of history. The philosophy of history is, as Hegel says, "to that extent a theodicy," and indeed "the real theodicy, the justification of God in history," of which Droysen still thought that "the highest task of our science is, after all, theodicy."[7] But this historical theodicy falls into an antinomy: *Without* progress (Hegel thought, and de Tocqueville also still thought, sadly)[8] God would not be just, because he would bar to human beings the path to the equal freedom of all; but *through* progress (Ranke and historicism[e] thought) God would also be unjust, because he would withhold from those who were born earlier what he furnishes to those who are born later; this is why, for reasons to do with theodicy, the concept of progress must be overruled by the principle that "every epoch has an immediate relationship to God."[9] Thus God, in dealing with history, has only the painful choice between two injustices (which exhaust all the logical possibilities): nonprogress and progress.

In view of this divine dilemma, autonomization quickly makes headway again in the nineteenth century, and with it the myth of the end of God: "The only excuse for God is that he does not exist," says Stendhal. Schelling (the later Schelling) had already looked for another excuse: God's ego has such trouble with his id [*Es*] that as a consequence God's omnipotence is curbed, he cannot prevent wickedness, and at the same time he indirectly authorizes man's autonomy, with the result that man ends up in the role of the redeemer of God. Since I read Peter Wapnewski on Wagner's "melancholy god," I can see that, by what we might call "another work on myth,"[f] Wagner only translated this basic pattern of Schelling's thought into the language of Germanic mythology, with a Wotan (in the *Ring*) who, as a result of guilt, has such trouble with himself that he has to let himself be redeemed by human beings, and consequently comes—with aesthetic pomp—to crave death.[10] This "twilight of the gods" did not go far enough for Nietzsche: for him, God "is" already "dead." That too, as Hans Robert Jauss and Hans Blumenberg have recently confirmed, is a theodicy. For Nietzsche thought that "God died of his pity for man."[11] Where there is pity and thus injury (the evils in the world) to be pitied, God is justified even in his own eyes only by his nonexistence, and man is thereby authorized in the autonomy of the superman. By this observation, I support my thesis that autonomization—of which the modern myth of the end and the death of God is a part—is a theodicy motive in modern philosophy.

Here, it seems, the successor of the Creator, who has either been relieved of his duties or has died, can only maintain himself, in view of the evils that (nevertheless) remain, by sidestepping them, into the role of redeemer: He goes into opposition not only to the old Creator of the existing world but also, ultimately, to the new one, and seeks—in an eschatologically revolutionary manner—the end of this world. This permanent flight from the role of creator into the role of redeemer—which soon came to be called "dialectic"—repeats (in theological or profane variants) Marcion's model of the two gods: of the redeemer who enters the lists against the creator. Thus when theodicy, the second refutation of Marcion, becomes the doctrine of autonomy, it ends up authorizing precisely what it wanted to refute—namely, Marcion; and that means that rather than protecting the modern age, it becomes the antimodern age: Theodicy, when it is radicalized as the doctrine of autonomy, flips over and becomes its opposite, eschatology. Consequently, if theodicy does not want to abandon the modern age, but to continue to defend it, it has to cultivate alternatives to autonomization.

The Theodicy Motive of Bettering the Bad

I wish to draw attention to one such alternative, while taking as my initial starting point a philosophy of autonomy: Kant's "critique." That critique is generally regarded as aprioristic. But that is not yet its specific character. Kant's critique is, more specifically, the apriorism that legitimizes a prioris as "conditions of the possibility of . . ." (in particular, experience): That is, it legitimizes them by functionalizing them. Thus its decisive justifying concept is "condition of the possibility of . . ."[12] This concept is not, as I myself assumed for a long time, original to Kant, but comes from Leibniz, who says in his *Theodicy* that God, in view of the optimal world, allows evil as the "conditio sine qua non,"[13] which in German and in transcendental German amounts to *Bedingung der Möglichkeit* [condition of the possibility of . . .]. The fact that, in this way, Kant's central justifying concept comes from theodicy, has important consequences. If, earlier than a prioris and other good things, evils were justified as "conditions of the possibility of . . . ," then they can continue to be justified as "conditions of the possibility of . . . ," that is, they can continue to be good—good, beginning with Leibniz, for the best possible world; good, beginning with Kant, for the best possible science; and good, beginning with Fichte, for the best possible history. The general principle in all of this is that evils can be good for something, and thus good.

Functionalizing evils is only one possible way of making them good, of bettering the bad; for this process is a part, a moment, of a general tendency in the modern world and modern philosophy, which is the great process of rendering evils no longer evil.[14] This process began, after optimism's "acceptance" of evils, with its crisis: There—where optimism was no longer satisfactory, and autonomization was not satisfactory at all—a way out was offered by the idea that evils are not so evil. Consequently (for reasons of theodicy) philosophy set out to save evils from their bad name, to liberate them from their traditional negative role and to assert their goodness. My thesis, then, is that this bettering of the bad—the modern process of rendering evils no longer evil—is a theodicy motive in modern philosophy. It takes place with every kind of evil. I can only suggest this here with five short observations.

Gnoseological evil is rendered no longer evil. Curiosity, which had been a vice, becomes the central scientific virtue; and error, above all, ceases to be evil. The fortunes of error show a rapid rise, in modern times, translating it finally—as "productive fiction"—into the positive status of one of the most important preconditions of cognition and of action, as "falsehood in a nonmoral sense" and "useful error" in the fictionalism (for which Kant prepared the way) of Nietzsche and Vaihinger. In Popper's view, *falsificanda* constitute the history of science: Our ascent is by means of errors. And fictions, it seems, are dominant throughout world history: Beginning with Marx, ideologies (necessarily "false consciousness") are regarded as historically potent, and, in Habermas's view, counterfactual imputations of humanity, as fictional anticipations of the goal, are the guarantors of dominance-free discourse. In my view, this positivization of what is fictive—which is a way of bettering the bad—derives from theodicy.

Aesthetic evil is rendered no longer evil. In modern times, the unbeautiful rapidly becomes a positive aesthetic value: we find alongside (and outflanking) the aesthetics of the beautiful the aesthetics of the unbeautiful—the sublime, the ugly, the Dionysian, the abstract, the negative, and so forth. This positivization of aesthetic evil presupposed the previous removal of the aesthetic realm from the status of an evil: The traditionally defective ("inferior") faculty of *aesthesis*— sensuality—advances, through the rise of aesthetics (after 1750), to the supposedly highest level reached by mankind, that of artistic genius. This corresponds to the general emancipation of what was traditionally inferior, which occurs on a broad front at the same time: the emancipation of emotion, metaphor, myth, the exotic, the savage, the child, woman, the third and fourth estates, marginal groups. In my view, all of these positivizations—as ways of bettering the bad—derive from theodicy.

Moral evil is rendered no longer evil. We arrive at the great process of "rendering wickedness no longer wicked" (E. L. Marquard), which again occurs, representatively, after 1750, following Rousseau: Man's natural goodness, we are told, is misconstrued by culture as wicked, and must therefore be rehabilitated against culture and its traditional norms. The wicked, Nietzsche also goes on to tell us, is in reality the good: The asocial is the creative, the alternative and deviant is the authentic, the antiauthoritarian is the vital, the anti-institutional is the humane, anticivility is strong in reflexion or in some other respect, the great refusal is the great liberation, revolution is the absolutely good act; and, from Kant to Bloch, the philosophical reinterpretation of the third book of Genesis supports this: The Fall is obligatory as the origin of freedom. In my view, this process of rendering wickedness no longer wicked by revaluing all values derives—as a way of bettering the bad—from theodicy.

Physical evil is rendered no longer evil. For in the same period effort and work are treated, for the first time, as positive; need is revalued, for example by Malthus, as the opportunity to conquer it. *Angst* becomes the feeling of authenticity. To this add the (early) disenchantment of pathology: Illness is uncoupled from wickedness and is no longer regarded as the punishment of sin or as a negative miracle; it becomes demythologized and objectivizable, in the period of the "birth of the clinic." A little later, being ill makes one interesting: It is a precondition of genius. Suffering is either revalued as positive, or repressed: Frailty is revered as existentially symbolic, or put in a nursing home; pain is celebrated as enhancing one's capacity for perception, or is anaesthetized; death (as Philippe Ariès has shown) is initially emphasized and then "banished"; in general, afflictions (the *mala physica*) are either promoted to opportunities or euphemized and concealed. In my view, this laborious positive revaluation also derives—as a way of bettering the bad—from theodicy.

Metaphysical evil also, and in particular, is rendered no longer evil. Finitude, in modern times, exhibits an irresistible rise and becomes—with, at the latest, Kant's proclamation of the independence of human and finite cognition vis-à-vis divine cognition—a positive ontological value, at the cost especially of what had hitherto been accepted as the preeminent ontological condition: that of immutability. Thus we arrive at the positive revaluation of mutability: The concept of a mutability that is no longer a metaphysical defect comes into existence (beginning, once again, in 1750, as Koselleck has shown) as the concept of "history," which—from the history of mankind to the evolution of nature—now begins its great modern career. In my view, this positive revaluation of the metaphysical evils of finitude and mutability derives—as a way of bettering the bad—from theodicy.

Of course, this great process of rendering evils no longer evil has to be carried out over the resistance of traditional norms, and this resistance is now regarded as evil, and the hitherto officially good things that generate the resistance are also regarded as evil: The positive revaluation of evil as good carries with it a negative revaluation of what was traditionally good as evil. Thus the modern bettering of the bad, which is a theodicy motive in modern philosophy, at the same time leads to a worsening of the good, which confronts us again with evils and thus aggravates the problem that it was, after all, meant to alleviate: the problem of theodicy.

The Theodicy Motive of Compensation

This is why still another motive—the last one I will treat here—gets its chance, and its importance, at this point: the idea that the evils that are present are at any rate adequately balanced by goods. "The Creator of nature," Leibniz writes in his *Theodicy* (and intends to justify him by this argument), "compensated these evils . . . with innumerable amenities."[15] That is the idea of compensation: Instead of counting on the evils' being made *good,* it counts on their being made *up for.* So my thesis is that this idea of compensation is a theodicy motive in modern philosophy.

It was able to become a theodicy motive because, in Leibniz's theodicy, the "old" nemesis nexus—according to which misdeeds are compensated, that is, punished, by evils—was turned around into the "modern" palliation nexus, according to which defects are compensated, or indemnified, by good things.[16] In this "modern" form, the idea of compensation inspires, from the eighteenth century well into the nineteenth, the balances that are industriously drawn up by philosophers of compensation, who seek to demonstrate that the evils in the world do not (as Bayle maintained) outweigh the goods, but rather the goods (as Leibniz was the first to maintain) outweigh the evils; or, according to an auxiliary theorem, the "maux" and the "biens" balance each other perfectly according to the law that "evils plus compensating goods equals zero." Robinet and the young Kant spoke of this law, and Azaïs (inspired by La Salle) went into great detail (in 1808) to show that in every human fate misfortune is so compensated by good fortune that the balance of fortune is always zero, so that all human beings are equal. In the course of the last decade I have several times drawn attention to the relation of these philosophies of compensation, in particular, to theodicy.[17] Now, in October 1981, Jean Svagelski has published an exceptionally thorough book on *L'Idée de compensation en France, 1750–1850,*[18] which supports this thesis and follows the relevant French conceptions of compensation up to Balzac. In the Anglo-Saxon countries, it seems to me, this theodicy-like drawing up of compensation balances is temporalized, by utilitarianism, into a task for the future: Intelligent compensation policy, aiming at "the greatest good of the greatest number," is supposed to improve the balance of goods against evils. This pragmatic compensating program of social reform continues to operate—in a form sobered by Emerson's "law of compensation," which expects an "absolute balance of Give and Take"—down to the present, in what Scheler called the "age of equalization" [*Zeitalter des Ausgleichs*]. In the German-speaking countries—where Burckhardt drew attention to "the secret law of compensation" in history, with whose "consolation" one must, however, "deal sparingly"—the compensation idea was sharpened even as early as Leibniz (and then energetically, after the crisis of optimism) into the *bonum*-through-*malum* or "good as a result of bad" pattern: Just as sin called forth the Redeemer, and thus became the *felix culpa* [fortunate guilt], so defects call forth compensations, and thus become opportunities. For example, it is true (*malum*) that man is a "stepchild" of nature, but it is just for that reason (*bonum*-through-*malum*) that he has language, as compensation ("covering his losses"). So Herder says, "In the midst of these deficiencies" lies "the germ of the substitute"; which sounds like Hölderlin, "Wo aber Gefahr ist, wächst das Rettende auch" [But where there is danger, the saving powers also grow], and Busch: "Wer Sorgen hat, hat auch Likör" [He who has cares also has liquor].[19] In the twentieth century, this sharpened idea of compensation, according to which evils are indirect goods and imperfections are opportunities, becomes (after its late passage through psychoanalysis, in Adler and Jung) a fundamental anthropological category. As a theodicy motive that has become unconscious, it governs, to a large extent, the contemporary philosophies of man and theories of the human. I offer two pointers in this regard.

First, in the foreword to the second edition of his chief work on anthropology, *Die Stufen des Organischen und der Mensch* [Man and the Levels of Organic Life], Helmuth Plessner writes about Gehlen: "His theses . . . can all be grouped around the idea of compensation, to which Herder attached the catchword 'creature of deficiencies' [*Mängelwesen*]." Man compensates for his natural deficiencies by means of "unburdenings." Sartre, too, thinks along these lines: Man has to compensate for his lack of prior essential definition by projects, by choice. But Plessner himself had earlier made central use of the concept of compensation. Man's "eccentric position" compels him to make compensatory attempts at recentering: "Man," Plessner writes, "wants to escape the unbearable eccentricity of his nature," and consequently "seeks compensation for his incompleteness, lack of equilibrium, nakedness," through culture, which is to say, through technology, expressiveness, transcendence.[20] What we can document in this way in Plessner, Gehlen, and Sartre (and which continues, in a subtler, generalized form, in Niklas Luhmann—the human system also, and the human system in particular, compensates for complexity overload by complexity reduction) has broad applicability: Contemporary anthropology defines men centrally as one who seeks refuge from his imperfections, and can only exist by means of compensations, as *homo compensator*. The modern and contemporary boom in philosophical anthropology takes place, representatively, under the sign of the idea of compensation, which is a theodicy motive in modern philosophy.

Second, only because that is so is it possible for new compensations to be discovered and planned in human affairs. "Compensation" becomes the slogan of current programs, such as the "compensatory fiscal policy" of Keynes and Hansen or "compensatory education" after the Sputnik shock. At the same time compensation has been made the key concept of the philosophy of modernization processes, by (for example) Joachim Ritter[21] and his school, according to whom the modern disenchantment of reality is compensated by the specifically modern development of the substitute enchantment of the aesthetic realm; or the modern artificialization of the world is compensated by the specifically modern discovery and apotheosis of untouched landscape and by the development of an appreciation of nature, including ecological consciousness; or the modern loss of tradition, as a result of incursions of objective thinking and of the increasing tempo of change in reality, is compensated by the specifically modern genesis of the appreciation of history—for example, in the form of the museum and of the human sciences [*Geisteswissenschaften*]. All of that, and much else, shows that the compensation philosophy of man is being extended, on all sides, in compensation theories of the human world. This confirms what I wanted to underline: that the modern and contemporary boom in philosophical anthropology takes place, representatively, under the sign of the idea of compensation, which is a theodicy motive in modern philosophy.

In this process, the original connection of the idea of compensation to theodicy is forgotten. Still, it is only logical that contemporary anthropology should take up a motive from theodicy, in particular. Not only is anthropology itself, as Werner Sombart was the first to point out,[22] a philosophy that is specific to the modern age. It also opposes the philosophies of history that desert, neoeschatologically, to the antimodern age. Because that is the case—because philosophical anthropology has the job of saying no to eschatology—it is natural for it to take up motives from the negation of eschatology that was the second refutation of Marcion: from theodicy.

Allow me to add one ultrabrief concluding remark. That a skeptic, such as myself, should give weight to theodicy—that is, to an exemplary metaphysical task—is only an apparent paradox. Metaphysics is the cognitive department that has problems with which it does not get finished; and theodicy is (as I think I have helped to show) an exemplary instance of this. To have problems with which one does not get finished is irritating for the theory of science, but normal for humanity. Skeptics, in my view, are the people who put up with irritations in the theory of science in the interests of human normality. For them, metaphysics—not getting finished with problems—is precisely not an opponent, but a human state of affairs, so that for skeptics, who opt for what is human, there can never be too much metaphysics. There are human problems in regard to which it would be antihuman, and thus an error in the art of living, not to have them, and superhuman, and thus an error in the art of living, to solve them. The skeptical art of not committing these errors in the art of living is metaphysics; and professional metaphysicians are people who have painstakingly and successfully learned not to get finished with problems. Here, precisely, is where their value lies. Of course, someone who gives no answer at all to a problem finally loses the problem, which is not good. Someone who gives only one answer to a problem thinks he has solved the problem and easily becomes dogmatic, which is not good either. The best thing is to give too many answers. That approach (for example, in the case of theodicy) preserves the problem without really solving it. There must be a thousand answers—perhaps, in the Orient, a thousand and one, and in Spain a thousand and three. Abstinence in answering and monism in answering are harmful; what is beneficial is an exuberantly debauched answer-life—which, for the most part, already exists, as the history of metaphysics, which consequently is the organon of skepticism. That is why the skeptic is enamored of the metaphysics that produces so many answers that they neutralize one another, reciprocally, and in just that way (divide and think!) leave the problems open, so that the experience of metaphysics, overall, is like that of the lion-loving lion-hunter who, when he was asked how many lions he had already brought down, could admit that the answer was none, and received the consoling response that with lions, that's already a lot. That is exactly what happens to metaphysics (which is why the skeptic likes metaphysics), and thus also to theodicy. The number of its problems that it has solved is none. But for human beings, that is already a lot.

Author's Notes

1. H. Heine, *Zur Geschichte der Religion und Philosophie in Deutschland, Sämtliche Werke*, ed. E. Elster (Leipzig and Vienna, 1890), vol. 4, p. 245 (= *Religion and Philosophy in Germany*, trans. J. Snodgrass [Boston, 1959], p. 102); H. Heine, "Einleitung zu 'Kahldorf über den Adel in Briefen an den Grafen M. von Moltke,' " *Sämtliche Werke*, vol. 7, p. 281.

2. I. Kant, *Critique of Pure Reason*, esp. B 116, B 697, A XI/XII. Cf. O. Marquard, *Schwierigkeiten mit der Geschichtsphilosophie* (Frankfurt, 1973; 2nd ed., 1982), pp. 60–61.

3. I. Kant, "Über das Misslingen aller philosophischen Versuche in der Theodizee" (1791), in *Gesammelte Schriften*, Akademie ed., vol. 8 (Berlin, 1912), p. 255.

4. Lactantius, *De ira Dei* 13.20–21.

5. H. Blumenberg, *The Legitimacy of the Modern Age*, trans. Robert M. Wallace (Cambridge, Mass. 1983), esp. pp. 126ff. Cf. A. von Harnack, *Marcion. Das Evangelium vom fremden Gott. Eine Monographie zur Geschichte der Grundlegung der katholischen Kirche* (2nd ed., Leipzig, 1924; repr., Darmstadt, 1985); and O. Marquard, "Das gnostische Rezidiv als Gegenneuzeit. Ultrakurztheorem in lockerem Anschluss an Blumenberg," in J. Taubes, ed., *Gnosis und*

Politik, Religionstheorie und politische Theologie, vol. 2 (Paderborn, 1984), pp. 31–36.

6. Cf. O. Marquard, "Idealismus und Theodizee" (1965), in *Schwierigkeiten mit der Geschichtsphilosophie,* pp. 52–65.

7. G. W. F. Hegel, *Vorlesungen über die Philosophie der Geschichte,* in *Werke in 20 Bänden,* ed. E. Moldenhauer and K. M. Michel (Frankfurt, 1969ff.), vol. 12 (1970), p. 540; J. G. Droysen, *Historik. Vorlesungen über Enzyklopädie und Methodologie der Geschichte,* ed. R. Hübner (Munich, 1958), pp. 341, 371.

8. A. de Tocqueville, *Democracy in America* (1835, 1839–1840; New York, 1946), vol. 1. p. 7: "To attempt to check democracy would be in that case to resist the will of God," because (vol. 2, p. 333) "it is not the singular prosperity of the few, but the greater well-being of all that is most pleasing in the sight of the Creator and Preserver of men. What appears to me to be man's decline is, to His eye, an advancement; what afflicts me is acceptable to him. A state of equality is perhaps less elevated, but it is more just: and its justice constitutes its greatness and its beauty. I would strive, then, to raise myself to this point of the divine contemplation and thence to view and to judge the concerns of men."

9. H. R. Jauss, *Towards an Aesthetic of Reception,* trans. T. Bahti (Minneapolis, 1982), p. 192, n. 17 (= *Literaturgeschichte als Provokation* [Frankfurt, 1970], p. 151, n. 17), has drawn attention to theodicy as the context of the following formulation: "But if one wanted . . . to assume that this progress consists in the fact that in each epoch the life of mankind reaches a higher level, that each generation thus completely surpasses the preceding one, with the last always being the favored one, while the preceding ones are only the bearers of those that follow them—then that would be an injustice on the part of the divinity" (L. von Ranke, *Über die Epochen der neueren Geschichte* [1854; Munich and Vienna, 1971], pp. 59–60).

10. Stendhal, quoted in W. Mehring, *Die verlorene Bibliothek. Autobiographie einer Kultur* (1944; Munich, 1975), p. 15. For Schelling, see esp. F. W. J. Schelling, "Philosophische Untersuchungen über das Wesen der menschlichen Freiheit und die damit zusammenhängende Gegenstände" (1809), in *Sämtliche Werke* (Stuttgart, 1856–1861), part 1, vol. 7 (1860), pp. 331–416 (the ground of the possibility of wickedness is "the part of God that is not He Himself": p. 359). On Wagner: P. Wapnewski, *Der traurige Gott. Richard Wagner in seinen Helden* (1797; Munich, 1982).

11. F. Nietzsche, *Thus Spoke Zarathustra,* trans. W. Kaufmann in *The Portable Nietzsche* (New York, 1954), p. 202; original in *Werke in drei Bänden* (Munich, 1966), vol. 2, p. 348.

12. Cf. Kant, *Critique of Pure Reason,* trans. N. Kemp Smith (London and New York, 1964), B 126: "The transcendental deduction of all *a priori* concepts has

thus a principle . . . , namely, that they must be recognized as *a priori* conditions of the possibility of experience."

13. Cf. G. W. Leibniz, *Theodicée*, in *Die philosophischen Schriften*, ed. C. I. Gerhardt (Berlin, 1875–1890; repr., Hildesheim, 1960–1961), vol. 6 (1961), p. 117; "Dieu . . . mais qu'il ne veut permettre le mal moral à titre du sine que non ou de nécessité hypothétique, qui le lie avec le meilleur."

14. Cf. O. Marquard, "Vernunft als Grenzreaktion," in H. Poser, ed., *Wandel des Vernunftbegriffs* (Freiburg and Munich, 1981), pp. 107–33, esp. 118ff.

15. Leibniz, *Theodicée*, in *Philosophische Schriften*, vol. 6, p. 409.

16. Cf. O. Marquard, "Homo compensator," in G. Frey, J. Zelger, eds., *Der Mensch und die Wissenschaften vom Menschen*, vol. 1 (Innsbruck, 1983), pp. 55–66, esp. 59ff.

17. Cf. O. Marquard, "Kompensation," in J. Ritter et al., eds., *Historisches Wörterbuch der Philosophie*, vol. 4 (Basel and Stuttgart, 1976), cols. 912–18; O. Marquard, "Kompensation. Überlegungen zu einer Verlaufsfigur geschichtlicher Prozesse," in K. G. Faber and Ch. Meier, eds., *Historische Prozesse*, Theorie der Geschichte, vol. 2 (Munich, 1978), pp. 330–62; as well as: O. Marquard "Glück im Unglück. Zur Theorie des indirekten Glücks zwischen Theodizee und Geschichtsphilosophie," in G. Bien, ed., *Die Frage nach dem Glück* (Stuttgart, 1978), pp. 93–111.

18. (Lyon, 1981). Svagelski's fundamental thesis is that in France the idea of compensation (in the context of the idea of equilibrium, symbolized by a scale or pendulum) is established and temporalized (by Formey, Robinet, La Salle, and Azaïs; in metaphysics by Malebranche and Leibniz; in politics by the theory of the European balance of power; in natural philosophy by Saint-Pierre, Buffon, Saint-Hilaire; in aesthetics by Balzac, among others)—but then it is destroyed by the triumphal march of the idea of progress (which is a development that Svagelski welcomes). While agreeing with the substantive results, in terms of conceptual history, at which he arrives, I would like to point out in reply to Svagelski's critique of the idea of compensation (his talk of the welcome "death" of this "monster") that a renewed boom in the idea of compensation must be the logical and legitimate result in contemporary philosophy as soon as the idea of progress enters its crisis, that is, especially after World Wars I and II. That is why a revival of the idea of compensation is in order today.

19. J. G. Herder, *Abhandlung über den Ursprung der Sprache* (1772), Reclams Universal-Bibliothek, no. 8729 (Stuttgart, 1966), p. 25; Hölderlin, *Patmos* (1803); W. Busch, *Die fromme Helene* (1872).

20. H. Plessner, *Gesammelte Schriften*, ed. G. Dux, O. Marquard and E. Ströker, vol. 4 (Frankfurt, 1981), pp. 24, 385, 395.

21. J. Ritter, *Subjektivität. Sechs Aufsätze* (Frankfurt, 1974).

22. W. Sombart, "Beiträge zur Geschichte der wissenschaftlichen Anthropologie,"

Sitzungsberichte der Preussischen Akademie der Wissenschaften, phil.-hist. Klasse 13 (1938), pp. 96–130.

Translator's Notes

a. See Arnold Gehlen, *Der Mensch. Seine Natur und seine Stellung in der Welt* (1940; 9th printing, Wiesbaden, 1972), translation forthcoming from Columbia University Press.

b. Hegel compared reason to a "rose in the cross of the present" in the preface to his *Philosophy of Right* (trans. T. M. Knox [Oxford, 1952], p. 12).

c. The contrast of *Gesinnungsschöpfer* and *Verantwortungsschöpfer,* "principled creator" and "responsible creator," alludes to Max Weber's distinction, in his essay "Politics as a Vocation," between (as translated by H. Gerth and C. Wright Mills, in *From Max Weber* [New York, 1946], p. 120) an "ethic of ultimate ends" and an "ethic of responsibility."

d. "Redeemer-men" versus "creator-men": As he explains toward the end of this section, Marquard sees the duality of "avant-garde" versus "bourgeois" as a variant of Marcion's Gnostic dualism of the redeemer god versus the creator god. See also the final section of "Accused and Unburdened Man in Eighteenth Century Philosophy," in *Farewell to Matters of Principle,* translated by Robert M. Wallace (Oxford, 1988).

e. On "historicism," see translator's note b to chapter 1.

f. This alludes to Hans Blumenberg's concept of "work on myth," in his book of that name (trans. Robert M. Wallace [Cambridge, Mass., 1985]). "Another" [*auch eine . . .*], in turn, alludes to Herder's *Another Philosophy of History for the Education of Mankind* (1774).

=== 3 ===

On the Dietetics of
the Expectation of Meaning:
Philosophical Observations

Sense—and this one ought to know—is always the nonsense one lets go. I think that as a philosopher contributing to a lecture series on "Meaning [or sense: *Sinn*] in the Horizon Established by Science," one should manage very well with this maxim, which (as you will have immediately realized) is a variant of a formulation of Wilhelm Busch's. Busch observed that "The good, and this one ought to know, is always the evil one lets go" ["Das Gute, dieser Satz steht fest, ist stets das Böse, das man lässt"]—which is reversed Plotinus. Rather than evil being a lack (*privatio boni*), good is a lack (*privatio mali*): It is the absence of the bad. That was Schopenhauer's thesis. Busch is rhymed Schopenhauer, by which I do not mean to assert that Schopenhauer's *lack* of rhyme is also a lack of reason.

I repeat: Sense—and this one ought to know—is always the nonsense one lets go. I would like to stabilize this formulation here (though from a position that is anything but Schopenhauerian) into a philosophical thought, and I hope to do so in the following four sections: 1. the modernity of the debate about sense or meaning (in the emphatic sense); 2. the deficit of sense or meaning and the mentality of claims; 3. the indirectness of sense or meaning, and the nonsense of aiming directly at sense or meaning; 4. a plea for unsensational sense.

The Modernity of the Debate about Sense
or Meaning (in the Emphatic Sense)

The following fact, to which the history of concepts and the history of problems attest, seems to me to be noteworthy: The problem of sense or meaning, and the concept of sense or meaning, in the emphatic sense (once a "hot issue," and now, again, a standing topic of discussion) are—in comparison to the traditional significances of the concept of sense or meaning, which differ from these—a very recent, and very much a late modern affair. One must or can, in my view, distinguish at least three concepts of *Sinn* ["sense," sometimes "meaning"]: the concept of sense that relates to sensuality, or "the senses"; the concept of sense (or "meaning") that relates to intelligibility; and the emphatic concept of sense (or "meaning") that relates to happiness. Allow me, first of all, to clarify these by making three brief remarks.

Sensuality

First there is the concept of sense that relates to sensuality: *Sense is what a person has who notices* (in contrast to a person who does not notice, because he lacks the appropriate senses, or because, perhaps as a result of orgies of abstract thought, all he does is talk nonsense), *and thus sense is what a person has who, by noticing, can enjoy or suffer.* Human beings notice by means of their five senses: vision (if they are not blind), hearing (if they are not deaf), taste, smell, and touch, that is, the ensemble of the senses belonging to human *aesthesis,* which is to say *sensatio* or *sensualitas* or *sensibilitas*—"sensuality" (in current speech), whose external senses can be distinguished both from inner sense (*sensus interior*) and from common sense (the *sensus communis* of the *communis opinio* [common opinion], of *topos* and "commonplace," and also of the common weal). Thus we have not only the "sensuous" (sometimes the "sensually gifted") human being, who enjoys by making the most of his or her sensuality, but also the "sensitive" human being who has a "sense for" something: a *Feinsinn,* an *esprit de finesse,* a faculty of sensing what is appropriate in terms of manners, the "fine distinctions" in this realm, and the tolerable possibilities of escaping from it into direct sincerity or rudeness; or a "moral sense" for the good; or "taste," "goût," "gusto," that is, a taste for what is beautiful; or a "feel," a "nose" for what is called for at a given time—which is a case that already obscures the boundary between the first and the second domain of meaning.

Intelligibility

For there is also the concept of sense (or meaning) that relates to intelligibility: *Sense is what something has that is intelligible* (in contrast to something that is completely unintelligible and alien). This is where, as another traditional meaning of the concept of "sense" (or "meaning"), the *sensus scripturae* or scriptural sense belongs—the possibly multiple (and, at least, both literal and spiritual) meaning of Holy Scripture. And here one can sometimes express the intelligible character and content of this or that text or action or reality briefly, in the form—and this too is a traditional concept of sense—of a "sentence" [*Sentenz;* cf. the Latin, *sententia*] (juristically, a verdict; practically, a decision; theoretically, a thesis; in literature, a motto or epigram; and metaphorically or emblematically, an allegory [*Sinnbild*]). All of these present a way of understanding something that is intelligible. This concept of sense or meaning that relates to intelligibility governs (and this too becomes a modern and hectic affair only in our century) the hermeneutic, phenomenological, and lately the sociological discussion of sense or meaning. The dispute in the neopositivist philosophy of science about the analytical criterion of sense or meaning (as a criterion by which to demarcate science)—the criterion that requires abstinence from metaphysics, as something "senseless" or "meaningless" in the sense of undecidable, unverifiable, untestable— is only the zero-grade instance of this discussion, which incidentally is able to stop the disastrous application of this criterion of sense to itself only by distinguishing between object language and metalanguage, a maneuver that always leaves open the question whether this distinction itself has sense in the sense required by this criterion of sense.

A more plausible approach is to regard those inquiries as senseless whose results have no consequences, such as, for example, answering the question whether the subtraction of the sum of all the digits of all the odd telephone numbers in Mainz from the sum of all the digits of all the even telephone numbers in Mainz produces a positive or negative number. "There's no harm in it, but what's the point?" would be the vernacular response, which thus employs the pragmatic criterion of sense. Just as what is correct is to be found within the sphere of what is worth discussing, so the definitions, predications, eidetic variants, shadings, and "involvements" of a thing are to be found within the sphere of possibility that is determined by its affinities. "The pipe is not an opera singer" is indeed true, but it is senseless, because it would never occur to anyone to say that it *was* one. This is the sort of thing that the phenomenological concept of sense or meaning has in view, up to Heidegger's superquestion of the "meaning of Being" and its characterization as time: It is senseless to characterize Being by features of what is present-at-hand or ready-to-hand, or their negations; in order to make sense, the understanding of Being, of the "is," always demands temporal characteristics, of which the official Occidental metaphysics—excluding the others—actualizes only one (so that that metaphysics is, in the realm of time, the coup d'etat of the present).

Understood phenomenologically and hermeneutically, the awarding of sense or meaning is, then, a process of demarcation: It illuminates the point of an actual position by pointing out what else, apart from it, could meaningfully be advocated, and by showing the boundary of what could not. This phenomenological and hermeneutic concept of sense or meaning lives on, in the work of Alfred Schütz and Niklas Luhmann, in contemporary sociology. I will spare you, on this occasion, a discussion of Luhmann's thesis that in negations, which combine reduction of complexity and preservation of complexity, what has meaning is what is actualized by the negation and what is potentialized by it (in any case, these two things, and only these two); because in this discussion, which people today like to conduct with excessive subtlety, one can manage very well simply by noting that the awarding of sense or meaning is a process of demarcation, which marks off the intelligible from the completely unintelligible, the familiar from the completely alien, the related from the completely unrelated, the possible from the completely impossible, the world from the nonworld. Here what is meaningful is not always also important; rather, the question of relevance leads to a third domain of meaning.

Emphatic Concept of Sense

For there is also the *emphatic* concept of sense or meaning: *Sense or meaning is what something has that is (if necessary, absolutely) worthwhile*—something that is important, that makes one fulfilled, satisfied, happy, and does not make one despair, something that is emphatically related, as their value and purpose, to human life, history, the world. This is the concept of sense or meaning that, as I interpret Mr. Saame's letter of invitation, is at the center of attention in this lecture series on "Meaning in the Horizon Established by Science." One could conjecture from this that this lecture series was organized to celebrate an anniversary, because—to the best of my knowledge—this emphatic concept of sense or meaning first saw the light of day exactly one hundred years ago, in Dilthey's *Introduction to the Human Sciences* (1883), and it did so as a critical term in warding off the theology and philosophy of history; for there, for the first time, we read that it is true that theology and (in "secularized"[1] thought) the "philosophy of history want to express the sense or meaning of the course of history, that is, its value and its goal"[2]; but in Dilthey's opinion "there is no more a final and simple word that would express the true sense or meaning of history than there is such a thing in nature"[3]: History has no "senso unico," it is not a one-way street. Schopenhauer's pessimistic suspicion that the world is meaningless had still been formulated without employing the word "*Sinn*" [sense or meaning], and it was Nietzsche who first used the term in this connection, first of all in *The Gay Science*[4]: "As we thus reject the Christian interpretation and condemn its 'meaning' like counterfeit, Schopenhauer's question immediately comes to us in a terrifying way: Has existence any meaning at all? It will require a few centuries before" [as a result of 'the rise of nihilism'][5] "this question can even be heard completely and in its full depth."

The raising of this question, in this emphatic form, is a specific feature of the late modern world, in which, admittedly, there are differing opinions as to how it should be answered—some saying, like Freud, that a person who asks what the meaning of life is is sick, and others saying, like Frankl, that a person who does not ask what the meaning of life is will become sick. In any case, the question itself seems to become increasingly unavoidable; one has to confront it—for example, in the form of the "absurd," as Camus puts it in *The Myth of Sisyphus,* where he says "There is but one truly serious philosophical problem, and that is suicide. Judging whether life is or is not worth living amounts to answering the fundamental question of philosophy,"[6] which is the question of sense or meaning; and in fact one answers it by "giving meaning to what is meaningless." This, at any rate, is part of the "defiant phase" of this modern boom in the experience of meaninglessness. A specifically modern experience not only in the cases in which it is articulated by means of the words "sense" or "meaning," it quickly enters the "lamentation phase": Then one laments the lack of meaning as the loss of meaning, by (perhaps) longing for the past times that did not yet have to lament the loss of meaning in this way, because—as religious ages, or ages that for other reasons were sure of meaning—they were able, with confidence in reality, to live, to hope, and to have faith, which now, we are told, is to a large extent no longer possible. Thus, in view of its loss, "meaning" becomes an emotive concept, which is how the modern and late modern discussion about meaning becomes emphatic; and that in turn makes the loss of meaning all the more painfully evident, so that what now seems a certainty becomes a widespread conviction, as well: that we late modern human beings live in the "nihilistic" age of the great meaning deficit. That is the state of affairs at present, the emphatic lamentation of the loss of meaning, which manifests itself additionally, in recent years, in various conspicuous phenomena: in protest movements (which sometimes articulate themselves politically) of those who feel the lack of meaning; in neoreligious movements, of a fundamentalist character, in search of meaning; in a widespread turn (also, and especially, in intellectual circles) toward old religious guarantees of meaning; in the (symptomatic) expansion of an advisory, care-providing, and therapeutic profession of "producers and transmitters of meaning," as Schelsky calls them; in large-scale philosophical jousting over the monopoly of the administration of meaning; and in the emergence of the question of meaning even among the so-called "individual sciences" and amid the squads of technological experts. People are wearing "meaning" again; "meaning" is "in."[a] Meaning becomes the standing desideratum; for apparently, in the world of today, an oppressive deficit of meaning is felt everywhere. How is this to be explained?

The Deficit of Meaning and the Mentality of Demands

Sense—and this one ought to know—is always the nonsense one lets go. This formula becomes the refrain of my reflections, here, because it can help to bring sobriety into the question of meaning. It seems to me that this question, having become emphatic and intoxicated with lamentation, needs some sobering up; and that is why I propose here to connect the problem of the meaning deficit—the great modern disappointment and lamentation about the loss of meaning—with our modern and contemporary mentality of demands.

I can already see you wearily shaking your heads. No. "We know that," you will say, "we have been through all that already; it is nothing new to us that our present-day society, with its preoccupation with demands, compensates for the deficit of meaning by its expenditure on consumption." This, you will insist, you have been told repeatedly already—that because the meaning of life has gotten lost, we flee to surrogates, and specifically to the mentality of demands. Our demands increase because meaning is not forthcoming: The modern welfare society is the (objectively futile) attempt to replace the lost meaning with luxury. Through a sort of "overkill"—that is, through "overlife"—the lack of meaning is transformed into a superlife. The place of meaning is taken by diversion, money, success, prestige, growth, corpulence in physical, technical, and economic forms: Modern society's preoccupation with demands is weight that it puts on in its worry about its deficit of meaning. Because the life that one lives is empty, one needs it, and everything in it, at least twice over: the second television, the second automobile, the second house, the second Ph.D., the second wife or the second husband, the second life (in the form, for example, of vacation). Recently this has even spread to the intellectual sphere, where there is (as Wolf Lepenies has sarcastically put it) an

increasing tendency toward second books. There are second profes-
sions, and second jobs in the shadow economy and as expansions of
sidelines; for example, someone who has long since had plenty to do,
with research, teaching, and scholarly administration, nevertheless
also continually takes on lectures, for example, as part of the liberal
arts curriculum at Mainz.[b] This mania for doubling is in fact going
around: Something that, if one lives it once, is meaningless, one has to
make up for (even if it continues to be meaningless) by living it two or
more times. Thus our demands on life grow in direct proportion to the
increasing deficit of meaning: Growth takes the place of meaning. "All
of that," you will say, "you do not need to make clear to us, because it
already *is* clear to us. We are already familiar with this connection
between the meaning deficit and the mentality of demands."

I assure you: I believe what you say. Precisely because I believe it—
because I suspect that you are familiar with this nexus of compensation between the deficit of meaning and surrogates for meaning, a
nexus that undoubtedly exists, and which I do not dispute—I would
like to draw attention not to it, but (extending this diagnosis, and only
in that sense correcting it) to something entirely different: to yet another nexus, which also exists, between the meaning deficit and the
mentality of demands. In my opinion, the following is the case. When-
ever expectations and corresponding results diverge, so that disappointments and experiences of insufficiency and lack arise, then there
is never only one possible explanation, but always two, namely: Either
the results are inadequate, or the expectations were too high; either the
supply is too small, or the demand is too great. That, in my opinion, is
also true in matters of meaning. The experience of meaning deficits
does not always have to be due to lack of meaning; it can also result
from excessive expectations of meaning. In that case it is not that
meaning is lacking, but that the demand for meaning is immoderate.
This second case, this other nexus between the meaning deficit and the
mentality of demands, seems to me to be the more interesting and
more important one. In the society that is preoccupied with demands,
it is not just that the demands compensate for the meaning deficit; it is
also that the meaning deficit itself arises as a result of demands, in the
form of an immoderate demand for meaning. Because we, the mem-

bers of the society that is preoccupied with demands, are spoiled by the repeated satisfaction of our demands, we want to be spoiled with meaning as well. That is why, in the society that is preoccupied with demands, the demand for meaning, in particular, climbs to giddy heights and beyond any level that can be fulfilled, so that this demand has to be disappointed, and thus inevitably produces the experience of lacking meaning and gives rise to the great lamentations of its loss. My thesis—which thus explains the loss of meaning as a result of the increase in the "demanding" attitude, in relation to meaning as well as other things—is, accordingly, this: *Our primary difficulty is not the loss of meaning but the immoderateness of the demand for meaning.* It is not the great lamentation over the loss of meaning that will help us, but only a "diet" in regard to our expectations of meaning.

This thesis cannot fail to provoke contradiction. It mobilizes resistance, and from at least two likely directions. On the one hand, it affects the professional suppliers of meaning; in particular, both those who make their living as paid mourners, in matters of meaning, and (to use a term of Max Weber's) the "hierocratically" inclined pointers-out of mankind's "senso unico" have to fear the loss of their jobs: My thesis attacks their line of business. On the other hand, those people (which is more or less all of us) for whom the loss of meaning has become the favorite alibi for expansive good living, or for grumbling about its absence, must also take this to heart. By means of an immoderate increase in demands for meaning, anyone could have a good excuse for laying claim to surrogates for the nonfulfillment of those demands: to a pleasant life, or to indignation over its absence. Now of course this all-too-understandable double resistance to my thesis does not make it false, but only underlines the necessity of formulating it explicitly and repeating it frequently, which I will immediately do once again: The modern and contemporary experience of the loss of meaning is a result of an excessive demand for meaning; so our primary difficulty is not the loss of meaning but the immoderateness of the demand for meaning, and we will not be helped by the great lamentation over the loss of meaning, but only by a moderation—a reduction—of the demand for meaning, which has grown immoderate: by a meaning diet, backed up by a dietetics of the expectation of meaning. "Dietetics" here does not refer to a branch of nutritional science, a very late meaning of the word. Instead, I have in mind here not, indeed, the original Hippocratic and medical use of this word, but the old one found in, for example, von Feuchterslebeng[c]: Dietetics is a part of practical philosophy. Its role there is not that of an ethics of diet—a "diet ethics,"[d] so to speak—but it certainly is a part of ethics. Instead of dealing with questions about the rational basis of norms, this part deals with the art of living—with suggestions, that is, for the art of living in a way that is reasonably free of complaints and reasonably happy. In other words, a dietetics of the expectation of meaning treats the question of how to deal with the problem of meaning in a life-nourishing way. I will offer some further thoughts on this subject in the two remaining sections.

The Indirectness of Sense or Meaning and the Nonsense of Aiming Directly at Sense or Meaning

Sense—and this one ought to know—is always the nonsense one lets go. This formulation asserts, among other things, that sense is something indirect; and so I will venture the following thesis in the dietetics of sense or meaning: The nonsense that one must most of all let go, for the sake of sense, is that of aiming directly at sense.

Sense, or meaning, is a pseudonym for happiness. It is not surprising that it comes into play, as a concept of what is worthwhile in life, precisely in the nineteenth century—at a time when (as a result of the success of the Kantian duty ethics of the categorical imperative, and its critique of "eudaimonism" or the ethics of happiness) the problem of happiness was banished, as a central positive problem, from philosophy, banished to such an extent that even where the problem of happiness reappeared (because in the long run one cannot banish the problem of happiness, as a central positive problem from philosophy), it was not allowed to appear under its own name, but only under pseudonyms, namely (to begin with, and again and again thereafter), as the problem of sense or meaning. This process of the pseudonymization of the problem of happiness is still characteristic of the contemporary philosophical scene. Consequently, in the intervening years, happiness has used, and probably also used up, a whole series of pseudonyms: "authenticity," "principle of hope," "undamaged life," "emancipation," "quality of life," "self-realization," and—again and again, in between these (and again today)—"meaning." Now, in the course of this process of the pseudonymization of happiness, we forget (perhaps not for the first time) something that is, in general, reasonably well known in the case of nonpseudonymous happiness: namely, that although, as Aristotle says, everyone wants happiness, it cannot be aimed at directly; and thus this pseudonymization of happiness, including its aliases, "sense" or "meaning," leads to the nonsense of aiming directly at sense or meaning.

By aiming directly at sense or meaning I mean an attitude that resembles the one that Hegel (in a different connection) illustrated with the little story of the man who wanted fruit, and who consequently spurned apples, pears, plums, cherries, and quinces, because what he wanted was not apples, but fruit; not pears, but fruit; not plums, but fruit; not cherries, but fruit; and not quinces, but fruit. And thus he chose the only surely successful way of not getting precisely what he did, after all, want, namely, fruit. For fruit, at least for us human beings, can be had only in the form of apples or pears or plums or cherries or quinces. A person who aims directly at happiness (pseudonymized as sense or meaning) fares very similarly, because what such a person wants is not reading, but meaning; not writing, but meaning; not work, but meaning; not lazing around, but meaning; not loving, but meaning; not helping, but meaning; not sleeping, but meaning; not carrying out duties, but meaning; not following inclinations, but meaning; and so forth. What he wants is not an occupation, but meaning; not a hobby, but meaning; not a family, but meaning; not being alone, but meaning; not the state, but meaning; not art, but meaning; not the economy, but meaning; not science, but meaning; not compassion, but meaning; and so forth. He, too, chooses the only surely successful way of not getting precisely what he does, after all, want, namely, meaning. For meaning, at least for us human beings, can only be obtained through an occupation, a family, being alone, a state, art, an economy, science, duties, inclinations, compassion, and so on, and to want to obtain it in some other way is nonsense. *No human being has a direct relation to meaning: Human beings always have only indirect dealings with meaning,* by the roundabout means of specific usual practices and tasks, which can also be (and very often are) institutionalized routines, and which, in any case, are always specific, and therefore limited, tasks. From which it follows, nota bene, that meaning, alias happiness, has to do with the ability to forgo things, which is something that the Stoics knew: He who cannot forgo things will not be happy. So, someone who wants meaning not by this roundabout means, by means of specific tasks, but directly, does not get it, at least not in this, our human world. In which case, he must want a different world, which is constructed in such a way that one can do there what one cannot do in our world: fulfill one's life by aiming directly at meaning.

One might think, then, that the nonsense of aiming directly at meaning might be one of the religions that promise that everything will become completely different—the religions that promise, like the Bible, a new world and a new human being in it. But here, I think, we have to distinguish between (in the case of Christianity), on the one hand, Christianity, and on the other hand, the positions in opposition to which it came into being by (early on) declaring them to be heresies. I admit, I do not consider it impossible that our contemporary need to be spoiled with meaning was promoted by Christianity, and specifically, when meaning as happiness was not so much pseudonymized as outbid by meaning as salvation, by the Christian assurance that God has promised human beings that they were not only (as in the Greek case, with happiness) included, in a finite way, in a good finite "deal"—in the polis, in the individual—but more than that, they were (in the Christian case, with salvation) included, in an absolute way, in an absolutely good deal, namely in God's deal. That is already a quantity of meaning by which one can become spoiled, in matters of meaning. But, I repeat, we have to distinguish: It is not Christianity that stylized this absolute meaning deal into an attitude that aimed directly at meaning; this was done by the positions in opposition to which Christianity came into existence by (early on) declaring them to be heresies. I am referring to the Gnostic-eschatological reading, advocated in its most logical form by Marcion, which—by positivizing alienation from the world, which it did by negativizing the existing world—opted for an entirely different and entirely new world, and consequently espoused, eschatologically, the end of the existing world, to such an extent that it also wanted the end of this world's creator god (that is, what we nowadays call the "death of God"), which would only be brought about by an antigod of redemption who would release man into a situation in which what is impossible in the existing world—fulfilling one's life by aiming directly at meaning—would be possible, and in which the principle holds that does not hold in our existing world: that human beings have a direct relation to meaning.

It is not only the Christian church and medieval philosophy that came into existence in opposition (and I am linking up here with theses advocated by Harnack and Blumenberg) to this Gnostic heresy and to relapses into it—an opposition that reestablishes, against the direct god, the indirect god, whom one honors by honoring, to an appropriate degree, his world and what human beings do in it. Ultimately, the age that was the initial subject of my reflections, the modern age, also came into existence to oppose this. The modern age too, and in particular—as the age of neutralizations of attitudes that aim directly at meaning—is a great attempt to restore the indirectness of meaning as happiness. This is done, if need be (though not always) in opposition to the God of religious eschatologies (when those eschatologies become, as in the wars of religion, the cause of direct quarrels about meaning, with bloody and lethal consequences), by taking the step into a profane existence, which neutralizes the religious factor. This step into the "age of neutralizations"[e] neutralizes the religious factor precisely in the sense that "neutralizing" has in six-day bicycle racing: When the state, modern (exact or hermeneutic) science, and the system of needs and its economic and technical articulations make their pragmatic decisions, nothing is decided any longer in the manner of salvation; and vice versa. This becomes unsensational, in its pragmatic sobriety, and (to that extent) a bit boring. Nevertheless, it does not by any means exclude meaning; rather, this sobering process, which is the modern age and its Enlightenment, only rescues—against every nonsensical direct aim at meaning—the indirectness of meaning. As a skeptic for whom the traditionalism that is part of every skepticism takes the form of a traditionalism of modernity, I maintain that it is important to recognize this sobering process (which is the raison d'être of the modern world) as reasonable, and, as Hegel puts it, to make one's peace with it—as a process that preserves what we human beings need: a process that preserves the indirectness of meaning.

A Plea for Unsensational Sense

Sense—and this one ought to know—is always the nonsense one lets go. A prime instance of this is the nonsense of aiming directly at sense or meaning, which, while it makes the problem of sense or meaning sensational, plunges human beings into unhappiness: into the experience of the void of meaning, into despair, and, in the extreme case, into a reversal of the direct aim at meaning—into the direct, demonstrative negation of meaning that is accomplished by suicide. These things— the individual's and mankind's aiming directly at meaning, and its negative counterpart, the individual's suicide and mankind's fear of suicide (its present-day fear of self-annihilation)—are the extreme poles of the sensational dimension of sense or meaning. Contrary to the basic tendency of the age of neutralizations, the tendency toward a pragmatic sobering of the world, to which the Enlightenment (when it does not return to nature) leads, and which thereby produces a deficit of excitement, of sensation—contrary to this basic tendency, it is precisely in modern times that this sensational dimension of sense or meaning is nostalgically sought out again and celebrated, so that it becomes a compensatory way of meeting the human need for excitement and sensation. This is accomplished, where sense or meaning is concerned, through the debate about sense or meaning in the emphatic sense, and through emphatic promises of sense or meaning and emphatic regrets about their absence, in which connection the promises or the regrets, and above all the sense or meaning, are secondary, and the primary thing is the excitement and the emphasis: the satisfaction of the need for sensation by means of sensational material (sensational sense or meaning, or sensational senselessness or meaninglessness), which results from a return to aiming directly at meaning or to directly and demonstratively denying it. This yearning for an emotionally all-encompassing supersense or supermeaning, one that is suitable for inscription on banners and for theatrical thunder, is a wave of nostalgia—compensating for our Enlightenment—in the grand style, and one that seems to dominate the late modern scene: a drunken yearning for sensational sense or meaning. But it is precisely this—this standing naiveté—from which we have to desist.

Therefore, the dietetics of the expectation of sense or meaning, which I am essaying here, recommends a *farewell to the sensational,* in matters of sense or meaning: a forgoing of sensational sense or meaning, and of sensational senselessness or meaninglessness—and consequently a forgoing of aiming directly at sense or meaning and of directly denying sense or meaning. That is, it recommends the cultivation of unsensational sense or meaning. Accordingly, it is concerned to reduce the expectation of sense or meaning from an expectation of direct sense or meaning into an expectation of indirect sense or meaning. In its view, then, it is necessary—now, in particular—for us to desist from at least four varieties of nonsense (and I emphasize: *at least* four, because my discussion makes no claim to exhaustiveness). They are: the prohibition of questions about sense or meaning; contempt for small answers to those questions; perfectionisms; and making the affirmation of life depend on an absolute proof of sense or meaning. In conclusion, I will make four short remarks, in sequence, on these four forms of nonsense.

Prohibition of Questions about Sense or Meaning

Today, especially, we have to desist from the *nonsense of prohibiting questions about sense or meaning* (for example, by the analytical criterion of sense or meaning, that is, the suspicion that metaphysics is senseless or meaningless). Consequently, despite my skepticism, I defend metaphysics, because metaphysics holds on to questions of sense or meaning. It is true that it does this by means of metaphysical answers; but sometimes one can only keep hold of questions by means of answers (often answers are, more than anything else, a means of transporting questions), and often questions of sense or meaning can only be kept hold of by means of metaphysical answers. In order, in accordance with the dietetics of sense or meaning, to supply questions of sense or meaning with moderate—perhaps (as the case may be) nonmetaphysical—answers, one must first of all *have* those questions; and it is better to have them metaphysically than not to have them at all, even if (in the skeptic's opinion) it is not always good to *answer* them metaphysically. But even from a skeptical point of view, metaphysical answers have definite advantages because as a rule metaphysics provides not just one, but several answers to a question—in other words, too many answers—and thus keeps the question open.

Contempt for Small Answers

Today, especially, we have to desist from *the nonsense of contempt for "small" answers to questions of sense or meaning.* Short of metaphysics, the minimal authority for a minimal answer, in the search for unsensational sense or meaning, is the experience of life. But this shows that just what the protagonists of aiming directly at meaning condemn as impeding and frustrating it—namely, the specific and detailed and institutionalized tasks of life, such as one's occupation, family, limited responsibilities, specific activities and routines—just this is the crucial remedy for what aiming directly at meaning inevitably turns into, which is absolute despair. Human beings do not despair as long as they always have something else to attend to: to keep the milk from boiling over, to drive the train to the next station, to feed the baby, to finish the operation, to write the recommendation for which the deadline is approaching, to give the stranger directions, and so forth. Thus, on account of these little delaying factors ("mini-katechons,"[f] we might call them), human beings, delayed (just as they ought to be) by their daily tasks, regularly arrive too late for their rendezvous with the absolute No. That is, quite unsensationally, the normal sense or meaning that our habits and activities give to our life. This small sense or meaning is sufficient in order to lead a life, and the great "Sunday" feelings—ecstasy, exaltation, transports of fulfillment—are, at most, *dona superaddita* [gifts "over and above" the necessary]. Grateful allowance can be made for them, if they don't create too much disturbance, but one can manage without them, too.

One lives so as not to make the lives of others more difficult; this, it seems to me, is the lesson that Guillaumet gives us,[7] who—having crashed his airplane in a wilderness of snow and ice that is hopelessly remote, for practical purposes, from human habitation—does not give up, but sets off to reach a place where his corpse can quickly be found, which is necessary so that his wife can collect his life insurance without the long waiting period that is required in the case of a missing person; in doing so he does after all, more accidentally than on purpose, come back alive. He was not concerned about the absolute meaning of life, but about the life insurance for his wife. To put it in an extreme form: In this situation, the meaning of his life was the life insurance for his wife. From which I would like to conclude that the answer to Camus's question "whether life is worth living"—that is, the answer to the question of the meaning of life—depends more on immediate things than on ultimate ones. (In religious language, one could say that God regulated this issue in accordance with the principle of "subsidiarity.") In Camus's book, this immediate thing, for Sisyphus, is his stone: Without the stone, he would have to despair; with the stone, "we must imagine Sisyphus as happy," Camus says, although this stone is only a stone and although for Camus it remains a stumbling block, a cause for revolt. Here I would like to depart from Camus: Our stone—our immediate things—is the ensemble of our small duties and habits in life, and as such it is, as a rule, not a stumbling block but a philosopher's stone. We are wise on just those occasions when we take care of these immediate things, because for human beings—for all of us—the question of meaning is not, as a rule, decided on fundamental grounds of principle. Instead, it is decided in part, indirectly and positively, by the care we take of immediate things—by our attention to details. Here, of course, and inevitably, we encounter the indignant question: And what role is left for critique, then? To which the answer is very simple: Critique, too, is attending to a detail.

Perfectionisms

Today, especially, we have to desist from *the nonsense of perfectionisms*. Among these, aiming directly at meaning is only the extreme case; there are also other perfectionisms. Hegel, in his critique of ethics of obligation,[g] drew attention to the fact (which I will formulate briefly, and consequently not at the height of Hegelian subtlety) that perfectionistic deontological demands have the effect of spoiling what exists. The demand that we should accept only what is perfect leads to discouragement and to feelings of meaninglessness: to the denial of the good in what is imperfect, and to the "infernalization" of existing reality. The claim to exclusiveness, on the part of what is perfect, attaches a negative sign to what is imperfect. For example, when one permits only perfect mutual understanding, achieved by the superpedantic observance of absolute standards of precision and by the superpedantic fulfillment of absolute duties to achieve consensus, then by that very means the existing mutual understandings—things that are taken for granted, usual practices, pragmatic conventions—are branded as senseless or meaningless, and the result is that the mutual understandings that are actually attainable are not facilitated but are actually impeded. Someone who is only satisfied with a supercommunication that is always perfectly successful, and who wants, moreover, to be in ongoing communication of the highest intensity with everyone, and expects even the statue in the next square to embrace him, and feels mistreated when, as is usual with statues, it does not do this— such a person, who excommunicates himself, in the name of perfect communication, from all actual communications, belongs among the geniuses in the production of despair, the masochists of meaning.

Against the perfection of all-in-oneness of mind [*Allsamkeitseintracht*] and group ecstasy, I plead for the soundness of the second-best possibilities in this domain: the hesitant smile, the little gesture, the transitory conversation, the helpful routine. Someone who accepts only the perfect world-improvement that, on the principle of "all or nothing," brings about the absolutely good world (for example, a world with an absolute structural guarantee of peace), and who wants nothing to do with the best that is possible, or the second best, infernalizes what is really possible and what is real; and since the existing world, in particular, is not the *ens perfectissimum,* "everything," it then counts as the *ens defectissimum,* "nothing." Since it is not paradise, it counts as hell (as though there were nothing in between): as something absolutely empty of meaning and calling for jeremiads. So the effect of perfectionisms is to spoil the meaning of what exists and is attainable, and thus, essentially, to raise potential distress to a higher power. The existing reality is regarded as infernal because the superbest is demanded and what falls short of it is discriminated against. But treating what is adequate as negative, in this way—making bad the good that is also contained in the existing, imperfect world—is something that we cannot afford: Finite creatures do not have so many irons in the fire that they can dispense with any of them. Just the reverse is the case: We have to keep our ability to perceive the goodness even of what is imperfect, and remain capable of noticing the "rose in the cross of the present," and thus we have to see that there is more meaning in the existing reality than the perfectionisms—which want to persuade us that what exists is empty of meaning—intend to permit. It is not that meaning is absent, but rather that on account of our increasing demands for perfection, our expectation of meaning is too high, and our tolerance for frustration has fallen, while at the same time we have a superexpansion of the techniques of complaint and of the art (pushed to a high level by the titillating effect of ideology critique) of being disappointed and switching from positive illusions to negative ones. As opposed to this, part of the dietetics of meaning expectation is muting perfectionisms by having the courage to be imperfect.

Absolute Proof of Sense or Meaning

Today, especially, we have to desist from *the nonsense of making the affirmation of life depend on an absolute proof of sense or meaning.* An absolute proof of sense or meaning—in the extreme case, the answer to the question, "Why is there anything at all, rather than nothing?" (which includes the question of theodicy)—is something that we cannot, absolutely, furnish: Our life is too short for that, because a limit is fixed to it by death. No negative attitude to life follows from this. Even if Silenus was right when he said that "the best thing is not to have been born," Polgar is even more right in his commentary on that dictum: "The best thing is not to have been born, but who does that ever happen to?" If we are already alive, then each of us, by living, has in some way assented—not indeed in principle, but in fact, and as a usual practice—to life. *Ex suppositione vivendi et ex suppositione moriendi* [assuming a living and dying creature], one would have to give reasons for departing from this practice of assent:

The burden of proof is on the negative side. But the same thing holds for the absolute No that holds for the absolute proof of senselessness or meaninglessness: We do not—vita brevis—have time, in our lives, to furnish it. From this I would like to conclude that our life has, in a very un-"principled," modest, contingent, and unsensational way, sense or meaning. That is, it has sense or meaning—it is worth living—not, indeed, because it has been proved to have sense or meaning, but because it has not been proved not to have sense or meaning: *in dubio pro vita* [in case of doubt, favor life]. That is so because our death is swift, which is why it always has an excellent prospect of winning the race, on the racetrack of our life, against principled despair. What else there might be to say about the meaning of life, perhaps by having recourse to religious material, seems to me not to be the business of the philosopher, or at any rate not of the skeptic, who has no mandate in that area.

With that, I conclude these reflections on the dietetics of the expectation of meaning, whose basic thesis was that we arrive at the great lament about the loss of meaning above all as a result of an immoderate demand for meaning. The primary problem is not that meaning is lacking but that too much meaning is expected. So this expectation of meaning has to be reduced by means of a dietetic plea for the unsensational sense or meaning that is left when one resists the nonsense of aiming directly at meaning and desists from the four kinds of nonsense that I discussed in the final section: from the prohibition of questions about sense or meaning, from contempt for small answers to those questions, from perfectionisms, and from making the affirmation of life depend on an absolute proof of sense or meaning. Thus I can sum up my reflections very briefly in, approximately, the statement that I began with: Sense—by now we nearly know—is always the nonsense one lets go.

Author's Notes

1. W. Dilthey, *Gesammelte Schriften* (Leipzig and Berlin, 1913–), vol. 1, ed. B. Groethuysen (1922), p. 99.

2. Ibid., p. 96.
3. Ibid., p. 92.
4. F. Nietzsche, *The Gay Science,* trans. W. Kaufmann (New York, 1974), p. 308. Original: *Werke in drei Bänden,* ed. K. Schlechta (Munich, 1966), vol. 2, p. 228.
5. Nietzsche, *Werke in drei Bänden,* vol. 3, p. 634.
6. A. Camus, *The Myth of Sisyphus,* trans. J. O'Brien (New York, 1955), p. 3.
7. A. de Saint-Exupéry, *Wind, Sand and Stars,* trans. L. Galantière (London, 1970), chap. 2, sec. 2 (pp. 38ff.).

Translator's Notes

a. In the original, "in" is in English, so the phrase reads: " 'Sinn' ist 'in.' "

b. This lecture was part of a series forming part of the *Studium Generale* or general liberal arts curriculum at the University in Mainz.

c. Ernst, Baron von Feuchtersleben (1806–1849), poet, essayist and professor of psychiatry in Vienna, was the author of *Zur Diätetik der Seele* [On Psychological Dietetics] (1838).

d. A pun is lost here: *Diät-Ethik/Diätetik.*

e. The "age of neutralizations" (*Zeitalter der Neutralisierungen*) is a phrase coined by Carl Schmitt in a lecture under that title, printed as an appendix to his *Der Begriff des Politischen* (1922, 1934; Berlin, 1963), pp. 79ff. See n. 34 to Marquard's "The Question: To What Question is Hermeneutics the Answer?" in *Farewell to Matters of Principle,* translated by Robert M. Wallace (Oxford, 1988).

f. *Kathekon,* the term applied by the Stoic, Zeno of Citium, to duty, is literally a "holding-back," a restraint or control.

g. *Hegels Sollenskritik.* See, for example, *The Phenomenology of Spirit,* trans. A. V. Miller (Oxford, 1977), p. 151: "What only ought to be, without actually being, has no truth." Marquard discusses this argument in his "Hegel und das Sollen," *Philosophisches Jahrbuch* 72 (1964): 103–19, repr. in his *Schwierigkeiten mit der Geschichtsphilosophie* (Frankfurt, 1973), pp. 37–51.

= 4 =

Universal History and
Multiversal History

History is much too important a matter to be left to historians alone. I think this is one reason why the topic of universal history has been assigned—here at the Albert-Ludwig University at Freiburg im Breisgau (of which I have the honor to be an alumnus, having received my doctorate here)—to the *Studium Generale,* the liberal arts program. It is a truly interdisciplinary topic.

Admittedly, the concept of interdisciplinariness is no longer one that inspires delight everywhere. Anyone who is in a position to listen to the grass growing in the collective thinking of the institutions that finance scholarly endeavors knows that in spite of some indisputably important results, the euphoria about interdisciplinary undertakings—which was a response to the negative aftereffects of the euphoria about specialization, which preceded it—has in its turn long since entered a period of disillusioned stock-taking. This sobering of interdisciplinary expectations (which can become an indirect opportunity for the *Studium Generale*) will certainly not lead to an abandonment of interdisciplinary activity, but rather to a change in its form. Probably this change will be encouraged by what the universities may be faced with in, at the latest, the 1990s, which is a return to the small university—an institution that perhaps no longer has to segregate so-called "high-level" research in institutions for pure research, but instead moves these tasks (now seen as "school" work) downward into collegelike circumstances, in which the new standard structure will be that of small departments with one professorship. For this process—in the age in which the consequences of the Pill are felt, and (accordingly) pressures to economize—will probably lead to a dismantling of the internal differentiation of disciplines, with a resulting reduction in specialization, so that the individual researcher will be trained to work also on a less specialized basis, going beyond his own discipline. Instead of expensive special "teams" for projects bridging disciplines, the primary agent of interdisciplinary activity then will again be the individual.

This is the individual who, as a wanderer between a number of scientific worlds, no longer lays claim only to the hunting grounds that are specific to his discipline, but also to a general poacher's license. In order to deal with my topic here, I will make use of such a license, and in doing so I am behaving very much as philosophers behave. For philosophy is not a speculative property belonging to the special sciences, and the philosopher is not the general secretary of their intellectual holding company; contrary to a widespread prejudice, he is no longer the one who is in charge of the "totality" at all, but something quite different, namely—analogously to a volunteer fire department (and not without a taste for the associated trumpets)—he is the one who takes on the superrisky semidetail in connection with which other scholars for the time being prefer, for reasons having to do with scientific respectability, to constitute the congregation of discreetly mourning bereaved ones, if the philosopher should suffer any misfortune in dealing with it. No longer the expert in regard to the whole, the philosopher is, rather, the specialist's stuntman: his double in dangerous situations. The topic of universal history (and its side topic, in a minor key: "multiversal history") is a topic that involves this kind of danger, so it is quite understandable that a philosopher should be sent ahead, in this lecture series,[1] to find out whether the attempt to disarm this explosive topic will produce an explosion; and of course it should be a philosopher from another university, because one has to conserve the local ones. I accept this role, and in accordance with it I will deal with four subtopics, under the following headings: phases of the program of universal history; conformism in acceleration; in praise of inertia; and in praise of motleyness.

Phases of the Program of Universal History

In the year of the French Revolution, 1789, Friedrich Schiller gave his inaugural lecture at Jena on the subject, "What is, and to what end does one study, universal history?" His thesis was that universal history was not a topic for "bread-and-butter" scholars, but for the "philosophic thinker," who throws into relief, in "the whole sum" of the "occurrences" in the course of the world up to this point, "those that have influenced the present shape of the world and the condition of the generation that is now alive." In other words, he is the thinker who defines history by its relation to the present and by its future goal, and thus introduces "a rational purpose into the course of the world, and a teleological principle into world history" which, therefore, Schiller thinks, "protects us from exaggerated admiration of antiquity and from a childish yearning for past ages," because, by "accustoming man to uniting himself with the entire past and to hastening, with his inferences, into the distant future," and by "transposing the individual into the species," it shows that "all prior ages have striven—without knowing it—to bring about our humane century," and thus to bring history close to its goal. Thus Schiller gave the classical definition of universal history, as the history that is universal because it turns all histories—all stories—into one, the single, unique story of mankind's progress and perfection.

Although world histories are being written even now, this definition of universal history has long since entered a crisis, and has provoked beautiful and sublime opposition, from Burckhardt's *Weltgeschichtliche Betrachtungen* [Reflections on World History], by way of Spengler's "comparative cultural morphology" (in *The Decline of the West*), with the affiliated theories of cultural cycles and the structuralisms that are its descendants, down to easygoing positions that reduce world history to, for example, the "world history of a few details,"[3] which Arno Borst essayed in his *Turmbau zu Babel* [Construction of the Tower at Babel]. Ernst Schulin's anthology, *Universalgeschichte* [Universal

History], documents the present state of universal history's definitional crisis and its aporias. In his introduction several aporias are diagnosed, of which (in my opinion) the difficulties about the "unified course"[4] of the process—the conception of a linear process culminating in the development of Europe—are crucial. I will return to these later. Schiller, like Hegel and Marx after him, did not yet see these difficulties, in spite of the immense ethnological working-up and popularization (which took place precisely in the eighteenth century) of the accounts of the voyages of discovery, and even though the Categorical Imperative in its famous formulation in terms of "ends" does, after all, prohibit regarding human beings of earlier ages merely as means of producing what we have at present and a future historical perfection, and thus denying them each their own particular historical path to humanity. Schiller, then, by not perceiving these difficulties yet, defines universal history before it enters its definitional crisis, by summing up (as we can see from Koselleck's concept-historical analyses) what had come into existence—true to the "saddle period,"[a] and with the assistance of the simultaneous invention of the philosophy of history—since the middle of the eighteenth century, from Voltaire and Turgot by way of Schlözer and Kant. His summation concerned "histoire générale" or "universelle," "allgemeine Geschichte" or "Weltgeschichte," "universal history with a cosmopolitan purpose," or precisely—as Fichte then says, as a "pragmatic history of the human spirit"—universal history: the supersingularized history that (to repeat what I have already said) is universal because it turns all histories, all stories into one, the single, unique story of mankind's progress and perfection. The discussion of universal history has to go back to this definition today, too, because, up to the present, it still has not been replaced by anything that is really satisfactory and generally acceptable. The development of its crisis proceeds, I think, in two phases, the phase of attack and the phase of self-defense.

The aggressive phase, the phase of attack—inspired by the rash political attitude, which the modern success of the state made possible, of thinking against the state while one lives from it—is the radicalization of universal history into the philosophy of revolution. If the present is not already almost mankind's perfection, it must be made so by force: by political overturning, by revolution, which is the action to which German Idealism—which, in its central inception, was universal history as philosophy of revolution—understood itself as a parallel action in the realm of thought. The crucial turning point in the self-confidence of the philosophy of revolution, and also the crucial caesura in the philosophy of German Idealism, is the revolution itself. The *realization* of the philosophy of revolution, first in the French Revolution and later in its successor revolutions, makes what was previously a hope, wish, or expectation an object of actual experience, and— because, as Hegel says, "absolute freedom" then becomes "terror," and the revolution becomes the hour of dictatorship—an object of actual disillusionment: We arrive at the great disappointment of the revolutionary "immediate expectation."[b] The immediate response of the philosophy of history—besides the discovery of an appreciation of history's indirect paths and detours, of historiographical "dialectic"— was, when confronted with a bad revolution in the present, to remove the good revolution *from* the present. For Hegel, the only good revolution now is a past revolution—in fact, the revolution before last, the Reformation. For Marx, the only good revolution now is a future revolution, and especially the revolution after the next one, the proletarian revolution. Or else—unless actual theories of downfall take the place of universal history—its aggressive, attacking phase comes to an end, and universal history moves from the phase in which it is a philosophy of revolution into another, second phase.

The defensive phase, the phase of self-defense, is led by this disappointment of the revolutionary immediate expectation to tone universal history down into a theory of evolution, by founding the philosophy of history in the philosophy of nature. For me, probably only because I happen to be somewhat familiar with this particular stretch of the history of philosophy, the paradigmatic event is Schelling's attempt, beginning in 1797, to cure the mischief that had become evident in history by means of "healthy" nature, which romanticism regards as the better history, and which consequently also has to be understood *as* history: "genetically," as (in Schelling's language) "impeded evolution."[5] In the context of universal history, that is the crucial thrust in the actualization of the trend of thought, beginning in the eighteenth century, whose origins Foucault investigated: the escape from classificatory thinking (an escape that Wolf Lepenies—contrasting Linnaeus with Buffon and his successors—described as the "end of 'natural history' "), and the transition to thinking in terms of development, whose stages in historiography have been compactly chronicled by Wolfgang Wieland in his article in *Geschichtliche Grundbegriffe* [Fundamental Historical Concepts] on "Entwicklung" [Development].[6] Darwin's theory of evolution makes this transition, so to speak, definitively successful, and its approach—which is a promising attempt to save the idea of progress by disencumbering it of its final goal, by forgoing teleology and absolute chronologies—also inspires (by way of Herbert Spencer) theories of social evolution as doctrines of the art of survival, some of which extol the right of the stronger, while others interpret the history of mankind as universal history in the sense that it continues natural evolution by more civilized means. Thus, this phase of universal history becomes acute when, to avoid sliding into the pessimism of theories of downfall, the revolutionary immediate expectation has to be extended into an evolutionary distant expectation. Indeed, this happens again and again, at intervals of decreasing length—a significant instance within the last quarter century having begun in the early seventies, after the disappointment of the revolutionary immediate expectation of the late sixties. In this case, in a way that is suggestive for universal historiography, there was a simultaneous advance of, on the one hand, the idea of the "long march through the institutions,"[c] and on the other that of the long march through the species and through the stages of mankind's social evolution. Thus, as a substitute for the original conception of universal history, theories of social evolution emerge (flanked by the boom in evolutionary theories of knowledge and ethics, such as those of Piaget and Konrad Lorenz, and in sociobiology, as taught by, say, Wilson)— theories of social evolution emerge that are developed sociologically (sometimes at a high level of abstraction and not without head-in-the-clouds transcendentalism) and in the neighborhood of philosophy, as in the work of Luhmann and Habermas. As a result of this transformation of the program of universal history into theories of evolution, we now live in the era of a second, more civilized Social Darwinism.

Conformism in Acceleration

Thus, what I have only sketched here begins—true to the "saddle period," as I said—in the middle of the eighteenth century. Since then, we have universal history, at least as a need and a program. Now the question that obtrudes itself is this: Why does the program of universal history arise precisely in the modern period, beginning in the middle of the eighteenth century, and why does it maintain its topical interest from then on, across more than two centuries? My answer—which is original in, at most, its simplifications—is based, at least in part, on truths revealed by my household idols in historical theory and penates in the theory of modernity, Reinhart Koselleck and Hermann Lübbe, whose work generalizes Burckhardt's theory of crises in his *Weltgeschichtliche Betrachtungen*. According to Burckhardt, historical crises are "accelerated processes"; in which case, the modern world, when it becomes, as a whole, a historical crisis, must be understood as an accelerated process.[7] Its rate of change increases, its tempo of innovation and obsolescence rises, its complication grows at an increasing rate; the tempo of alteration in conditions of life (the dismantling of familiar things and the production of strange ones) advances; everything is in flux, and at greater and greater speeds. This creates a need for mastering acceleration. Now, my thesis is that universal history—whether it is being set in motion by the philosophy of history, radicalized as a revolutionary doctrine, or tempered as an evolutionary one—is an attempt to master acceleration through acceleration conformism. This is evident, I think, from at least four distinctive characteristics of the phenomenon, to which I would like to draw attention here by four brief remarks.

Mutability

A premise of universal history, both revolutionary and evolutionary, is the assignment of a positive ontological value to mutability. That is not something that goes without saying, because premodern tradition had imputed ontological goodness only to the immutable, to that which invariably remains the same as itself; and mutability counted, ontologically, as evil, as the *malum metaphysicum*. But when—beginning with

Leibniz's *Theodicy* at the outset of modernity—one no longer wants to blame God for evils, one is logically forced to assign a positive value to the evils that he has "permitted," including the *malum metaphysicum*. The latter takes part in the great, characteristically modern process by which evils are rendered no longer evil. Hence we have, since the eighteenth century, the upward promotion of finitude, as well, which is part of the ontological ennoblement of mutability, which in turn leads to history's immense gain in importance, by which we adapt ourselves to the modern accelerated mutability of the world. When everything is in flux, continuance, as an ontological standard, ultimately dissolves too, and mutability becomes ontologically positive—initially, in the forms of progress and development. Of the necessity of change we make the virtue of history, and the universal virtue of universal history: through acceleration conformism.

Transiency

In an extended version of universal history, and especially of the philosophy of revolution, the *malum metaphysicum* of mutability (and thus also of transiency), which is positivized as history, turns out to have an additional good quality. For, it seems, the evil of transiency guarantees the transiency of evils and is thus itself all the more a good, so that it must now be welcomed and pressed forward all the more, by universal history, as an additional acceleration in the interest of progress. Consequently one seeks, by increasing the tempo of the completion of history, a shorter and shorter gap between history's present state and its completion; and the shortest gap between the two of them is, apparently, revolution. So revolution is the really good evil, the epitome of the final evil that definitively removes evils. The metaphysical ultraevil becomes the historical superbest as a leap into the consummating end of history, which universal history extols and trains for. Of the necessity of accelerated change we make the virtue of revolution: through acceleration conformism.

Long-term Trends

Part of universal history, both revolutionary and evolutionary, is its tendency to reach out to great, and ever greater, temporal dimensions:

One increasingly needs the confirmation that is provided by a long-term "trend." When mutability is given a positive value and acceleration of tempos becomes a historical duty, the turbulences of the present increase, and now (when the ontology of the immutable is no longer intact) one can only deal with this by falling back on a temporal transcendence: on a past that was already the path to the only correct future. The current turbulences and confusions about one's direction have to be understood as a segment of a long history that is common to all, so that one can endure them and preserve one's confidence that one is on the right historical track oneself. The more turbulent the turbulence of the moment is, the longer the long history has to be to accomplish this: Ultimately one reaches beyond the history of mankind and the evolution of living things and back to the original cosmic explosion, in order to confirm that, despite everything, one is in line with and correctly continuing the universal trend. Of the necessity of present confusion we make the virtue of our total universal-historical orientation: through acceleration conformism.

Surpassing in Acceleration

Part of universal history—and it is just this that compels its revolutionary version continually to "repristinize" itself, over against its evolutionary version—is the phenomenon of "surpassing in acceleration," which is the law of the historical avant-garde. This is connected with the modern tribunalization of historical lived reality. For where, as universal history sees it, human beings more and more make their history themselves, they take over from God not only his role as creator but also his role as the defendant in connection with theodicy. Inasmuch as evils continue to exist in the world, the only prospect of exculpation in connection with them—by this tribunal before which it is no longer God, but human beings who are accused by human beings—now lies in being assured that while it is human beings who are responsible, it is always only the other human beings. In proof of this, then, these other human beings have to answer (as the slow human beings who resist the increasing tempo of the process of history) for the present state of affairs, being identified and condemned to immediate pastness by the historically swift human beings who claim (with universal history's guarantee that they are among the definitive victors in history) to be agents of the good future, already, in the present. Human beings escape indictment for the evils of the present by becoming its avant-garde, because the avant-garde, which is always swifter than the indictment, escapes the tribunal by becoming it: by flight into issuing indictments (flight from *having* a conscience into *being* the conscience), which is a faster and faster "flight forward." Of the necessity of acceleration they make the virtue of surpassing in acceleration, which makes universal world history into the last judgment and the avant-garde into its judges: through acceleration conformism.

My intention, with these four remarks (remarks that need further detail, which could be provided), was to explain the thesis that I had formulated as follows: Universal history, whether it is set in motion by the philosophy of history, radicalized as a revolutionary doctrine, or tempered as an evolutionary one, is the attempt—which is part of the modern world—to master acceleration through acceleration conformism.

In Praise of Inertia

Thus universal history, as the theory of the emancipatory revolutionary avant-garde and as the theory of social evolution, proclaims man to be a triumphant creature: the victorious protagonist of the realm of freedom or at least the current wearer of the yellow jersey in the *tour de l'évolution,* the world championship of survival.[d] But the end result in every case is that human beings triumph by triumphing, at the same time, over human beings, because universal history (insofar as it is inspired by acceleration conformism) is always driving at a finale in which human beings are compelled to deny humanity to other human beings, and thus to become, themselves, inhuman. Universal history, under the sign of acceleration conformism, always runs the risk of losing humanity in its effort to serve mankind. There is a maxim that warns against this, and with which I have not yet sufficiently provoked my fellow human beings, so that (in the interests of economy in provocation, as well) it is worthwhile repeating it here, and in the following version, in particular: He who wants to be human would do better to be inert than to be universal.

This maxim is meant to promote, contrary to every acceleration conformism, the humane goodness of systems or conditions that are "alteratively inert" in history. These include, and are founded on, constants,
such as the "never-changing riddles of life" which Wilhelm Dilthey
listed: "birth, reproduction, death."[8] But the realm of the alteratively
inert also includes precisely all the many things that only change slowly,
and indeed at least (and I emphasize at least) so slowly that the result of
the change does not affect the same generation that saw its beginning.
The rule, in relation to all these alteratively inert things, is that what is
antiquated by historical changes and accelerations of change is not
inhuman, but rather, for the most part, distinctively human—and I
include in this the "all-too-human," and (in the modern world) the
"antiquatedness of man," which Günther Anders laments in view of
"Promethean shame."[e] What is human is the ritardando. Universal history cannot assert this humane goodness of what is alteratively inert, in
history—of the stories of where we come from, which are threatened
with obsolescence by the accelerating story of where we are going—
because its thinking is acceleration conformist; so we need different
organs for that, which include (in my opinion) philosophical anthropology, together with its (since Herder and Dilthey) classical coalition
partner, the historicism that is mindful of motleyness.[f]

In my concept-historical investigations, the first of which was published in 1963, I have attempted (initially from a very different value
perspective) to show that philosophical anthropology, as a philosophy
of man's "nature" and of his constant and alteratively inert conditions, is established precisely in opposition to the philosophy of history: in opposition, that is, to the universal history that goes with the
philosophy of history. Today, in view of the boom in evolutionary
theories, I have to add that this opposition continues in the form of at
least a problematic relationship between philosophical anthropology
and the doctrine of evolution. The initial philosophical anthropologies
of our century—the anthropologies of Scheler, Plessner, and Gehlen,
which ascribed to man a special position in nature—adopted a neutral
attitude toward Darwinism (for example, by falling back on the model
of layers). Wolf Lepenies has some thoughts that, to me at least, suggest why this should have been the case.[10] He suggests that while on

the one hand the doctrine of evolution—which (in a way that is perfectly consistent with philosophical anthropology) associates man in the closest possible way with nature—made anthropology (as an integrated overall science of man) possible in a way that it had never been before, at the same time it made it superfluous, and thus institutionally nonexistent. This is because, for natural evolution, as Darwin remarked, "man is no exception"; so that it was not anthropology but biology that institutionalized itself in the nineteenth century, by turning man's special characteristics over to belles-lettres, with which philosophical anthropology (in romanticism and in the twentieth century) associated itself. Anthropology, with its opposition to the philosophy of history, fell apart into biology and belles-lettres.

Here, naturally, attempts at reconciliation are indicated, and the most recent one that I am acquainted with is Günter Dux's new book on the *Logik der Weltbilder* [Logic of World Pictures].[11] It defines man, in what at first seems a perfectly unexceptionable way, as a continuation of evolution by means involving autonomy (which is to say, by means of history), and then asserts, as its key thesis, that the natural compulsion by which man (as a result of the reduction of his instincts) has to invent himself freely through learning, is repeated in every human ontogenesis as the "cultural zero point" that is represented by the birth of each human being, which then is surpassed (to varying degrees in various cultures) only in the process of growing up. The rule for every human being, as a result of every birth, is that he or she first exists and then invents himself or herself. So, according to this evolutionary existentialism of Günter Dux's, beginning at least many tens of thousands of years ago every human baby—condemned to freedom and to his or her mother—has been a little Sartre and a potential late European, for whom we need a special explanation as to why he or she does not immediately escape the matromorphic perspective on the world, which Dux calls the "subjective schema," but only does so in the late European modern age, and why in other cultures, in spite of his or her equal opportunity for freedom at birth, he or she falls (to varying degrees) short of this. For Dux, the retarding factor (which plays the role, for him, that "fantasy" plays for Comte) is the "subjective schema" itself, which operates as a "barrier." Thus, if I understand this correctly (and Mr. Dux may correct me and rake me over the coals in his lecture, later in this series), the peculiarities of the various cultural formations are deficiencies, because they are products of the retardation of a history that in itself delights in progress and acceleration. That is, in Dux's work universal history's model of linear progress prevails, in a way that is consistent with acceleration conformism, over the appreciation of constants that goes with his anthropological starting point.

The reason for this is, I think, that among the "riddles of life," Günter Dux takes as his leading anthropological constant only "birth," which does indeed open up prospects of freedom, and not also "death," which limits freedom and does so by fixing a limit to life, making us poor in terms of lifetime. In contrast, I would like—as is not inappropriate for a philosopher who, through his Doktorvater Max Müller, is an academic grandchild of Heidegger (and still less inappropriate when he is speaking here, in Freiburg)—I would like to assign some priority to death. Human beings exist "toward death,"[12] though in a completely unemphatic sense, which I can describe (in line with the philosophy of the scarcity of the resource of lifetime, which is also a philosophy that one can find in Heidegger) as follows. Like their natality, the mortality of the total human population amounts, as it always has, to 100 percent, and as human beings we know this, so that the rule is that, vita brevis, we do not have enough time continually to invent everything from scratch, but we always have to fall back, for the most part, on what already exists and is accepted. Nor, vita brevis, do we have enough time to put in question and to alter, to whatever extent we might like, what already exists and is accepted; so that we must always, for the most part, continue what already exists and is accepted. For we are condemned, by our births, not only to freedom but also to death: Life is short, so that— as creatures who inevitably are alteratively inert—we have to link up with things that already exist. The latter are always contingent special circumstances, not, however, in the sense of arbitrary things that can be selected or rejected arbitrarily, but rather in the sense of fates that can hardly be escaped: The choice that we are[g] is always sustained by this nonchoice that we are; human initiative requires hu-

man inertia. Consequently—that is, because we die—we are alteratively inert and we die if too much change is demanded of us.
Someone who forgets this—say, by demanding too much dismantling
of particularities, or too much obligatory universalization—such a
person forgets, with ruinous consequences, what is human. For man
is inescapably, as a result of his mortality, the alteratively inert creature who has to link up, the *zoon hypoleptikon*,[h] which *can be* the
animal that draws inferences [*schliessen*], because it is the animal that
has to connect [*anschliessen*] with prior givens. So the rule, I repeat,
is that he who wants to be human should always be more inert than
universal.

It is only apparently the case that it is all over with this human
alterative inertia in the modern world, on account of today's acceleration of change. This is only apparent because—and we could call this
the "cunning" of inertia—the modern acceleration of change itself
enters the service of alterative inertia. What I described initially (with
reference to Koselleck and Lübbe) really is the case: The tempo of
innovation and the speed with which things become obsolete do increase in modern times. This is why nowadays we are all the ones
who—but just this is human—can no longer quite keep up, and who,
as a rule, also know this, when we do not conceal our knowledge by
means of acceleration conformisms. However, and this seems to me to
be important, part of the increasing speed with which things become
obsolete in the modern world, is the increasing speed with which the
obsolescence of these things becomes obsolete. The result is that the
faster the new becomes the old, the faster the old again becomes the
new. Thus the slowness and retardation that inertia produces becomes
an opportunity: Under conditions of acceleration, methodical out-of-
dateness may in fact be, for human beings, the most promising strategy
for always being maximally up to date. If, as a result of mortality, the
resource of alterability, in humans, always remains a scarce one, then
the faster the tempo of the long-distance race called history becomes,
the more one should calmly allow oneself to be out-distanced, and
wait until the course of the world completes a lap and catches up with
one again. Then one will again be accepted as the "cutting edge"—in
passing, at shorter and shorter intervals, and just as erroneously as

effectively—by those who believe in avant-gardes at all. This is how it comes about, as everyone who has been around only a little longer can attest, that what was just definitively outmoded reappears again, at shorter and shorter intervals, with or without fashionable camouflage, as the newest thing. Thus we now have the waves of nostalgia, from Neo-Marxism by way of systems theories and evolutionary theories to the new Orientalism and the Neo-Rousseauism of the Greens: The obsolescence of these things became obsolete. The art of noticing processes like these is the sense of history, which is able to draw attention (thus compensating for acceleration conformism) to the fact that in modern times the increasing speed of obsolescence is compensated by an increase in the likelihood that old things will be reactivated. Thus in history—the eternal recurrence of what is not the same—its contemporary acceleration is itself a continuation of the eternal recurrence of the same by the most modern means: The modern acceleration of change is an agent of human alterative inertia.

In Praise of Motleyness

To that extent, something that I regard—perhaps still much too naively, by the standards of scientific historiography—as the quintessence of our experience with history may (under the sign of the coalition between philosophical anthropology and historicism that I mentioned earlier) hold true. Namely, that only our initial experience with history (an experience through which, admittedly, all of us must pass) is of how much has changed even in places where almost nothing has changed; and that our second and more lasting experience with history is of how little has changed even in places where almost everything has changed. A sense of history is above all a faculty for perceiving instances of inertia. The basic experience of historical matters is, in my view, not so much the experience of changeability as the experience of the limits to that changeability.

What this means is that even if historical changes really do tend, in the long run, toward the universal, history always persists (on account of this inertia) in the nonuniversal—in the motley particulars—to a greater degree than universal history thinks its does; and this, in my opinion, is good. Mortality causes alterative inertia; alterative inertia preserves motleyness; and without this motleyness we could not live. Even when, in modern times, human affairs are interdependent on a worldwide scale, so that global—universal—regulating processes become inescapable, these universals do not regulate precisely what is most important in life. This is the case, for example, when (universalistically, and desirably) all human beings are recognized as being equal; for of course equality means the right of everyone to be different without fear. That is why the more important thing, for human beings, is not their capacity for generalization but their capacity for particularization: their "motleyness competence"; and every universalization has to promote motleyness, or it is good for nothing.

In my opinion, the classical definition of universal history—as the supersingularized history that is universal because it turns all stories into one, the single, unique story of mankind's progress and perfection—overlooked just this. Someone who defines history as the long march into the universal and as the path of the individual's dissolution into the species must logically assume, to repeat the passage from Schiller that I quoted earlier, that "all prior ages have striven . . . to bring about our humane century" and thus to bring history close to really existing universality; he thus becomes a kind of "committed" reporter, who—as a sort of William Tell, but equipped with microphone and camera rather than crossbow and arrow, and rejoicing and inciting, rather than lying in wait—reports, regarding mankind in its present, late European phase: "It has to pass through this narrow passage. There is no other path to freedom. Here mankind will complete its task, and necessity is on its side." Fundamentally, this conviction is still involved, though in an attenuated form, in the famous first sentence of Max Weber's *Gesammelte Aufsätze zur Religionssoziologie:*

> A product of modern European civilization, studying any problem of universal history, is bound to ask himself to what combination of circumstances the fact should be attributed that in Western civilization, and in Western civilization only, cultural phenomena have appeared which (as we like to think) lie in a line of development having *universal* significance and value.[13]

Of course, in Schiller's classical definition of universal history the tone was less cautious: There, the only interest in what went before was as a means of self-confirmation by the present. It has to be admitted that this instrumentalization of historical material by universal history is a forgetting that is disguised as remembering. In his *Structural Anthropology*, Claude Lévi-Strauss protested against this attitude—and extended Ranke's thesis of the equal opportunity of all epochs into a thesis about the equal opportunity of all cultures—with, among other propositions, one that sounds as though it had been formulated as a direct response to Schiller. "A society," Lévi-Strauss writes,

> can live, act, and be transformed, and still avoid becoming intoxicated with the conviction that all the societies which preceded it during tens of millenniums did nothing more than prepare the ground for *its* advent, that all its contemporaries—even those at the antipodes—are diligently striving to catch up with it, and that the societies which will succeed it until the end of time ought to be mainly concerned with following in its path.[14]

Instead, in the opinion of this critique of the "myth of the French Revolution," there are many individual paths to humanity. Consequently there can be—liberaliter—not just one unique history; instead, there must be many histories. What is more important than universal history is the reply to it that promotes motleyness, which (if, to produce a convenient formula, we have to stick to the linguistic singular) is "multiversal history," the scholarly form of polymythical thinking.[i] Universal history is human only insofar as it functions, directly or indirectly, to empower multiversal thinking.

Which implies, I think, that universal history is only made human by historicism—that is, by the self-distancing procedure by which the late-European sense of history can allow human beings, all of them together and each of them individually, to have not just one history (or story) but many histories (or stories), in which they are entangled and which they can and must tell; because for human beings—and this brief double reflection will serve to conclude my discussion here—that is just as necessary as it is possible.

It is *necessary* for human beings to have not only one unique history or story, or a few of them, but many of them. For if they—each individual human being, and all of them together—had only one unique history or story, they would be utterly in the power and at the mercy of this sole history or story. Only when they have many histories or stories are they freed, relatively, from each story by the other ones, and thus able to develop a manifoldness that is, in each case, their own—that is, able to be an individual, be it only a desperate individual, who knows that only one thing *really* helps him to get past one desperate situation, and that is the next one. Since finite creatures, on account of their mortality, cannot define themselves *ex nihilo,* they are free only—*divide et fuge!* [divide and escape!]—by virtue of the separation of powers: by virtue also, ultimately, of the separation of the powers that histories or stories are, and by virtue even of the separation of the powers that the tellings and interpretations of histories and stories are. They are free, that is, by virtue of the separation of one history or story into many. Here the history of universalizations is one history among others: Universal history is a history to which we can assent only if it is ready to be not the only history, but one—and by no means the most important—history among others.

At the same time, it is also *possible* for human beings to have not only one unique history, and not only a few histories or stories, but many of them—in spite of the harsh compulsion to singleness that we are all subject to because we have only one single life. For this *vita una* argument, which Eckhard Nordhofen has brought into play,[15] seems to me to be less an objection than a starting point for a philosophy of the human need for fellow human beings. For if, as is indeed the case, each of us has only one single life, but has to have a number of lives in order really to have many histories or stories, then we need the others, our fellow human beings, of whom there are in fact a number, and who consequently lead a number of lives. Communication with others is the only way for us to have a number of lives and thus to have many histories or stories; and I am speaking not only of simultaneous communication with other people who live at the same time we do, but also of historical communication with other people of other times and alien cultures, in which it is precisely their motley differentness from us that is needed and is important, and must therefore not be expunged, in our communication with them, but fostered and protected. Of course that distinguishes this (so to speak) multiversalistic communication from the universalistic communication that Apel and Habermas picture as the ideal discourse, for in the ideal discourse (which is an analogue of universal history) motleyness is permitted only as the initial constellation, motion is justified only as the dismantling of motleyness, and the goal state—the universalistic consensus—is a state in which no one remains different from the others, so that then, fundamentally, all the participants become superfluous, except for the one participant who suffices to cherish the opinion that then reigns, in any case, as the only one. Thus in the end the transcendental solipsism that the model of the ideal discourse as communicative action was invented to oppose catches up with this discourse again: The discursive consensus itself is the revenge of solipsism on the discourse that was supposed to overcome it. For, as the goal of the histories or stories in universal history is for the histories or stories to become superfluous, so the goal of the participants in the ideal discourse is for the participants to become superfluous. This universalistic communication, then, is not the same as multiversalistic communication, the communication of the endless conversation, which needs and preserves the differentness of the others. Multiversalistic communication is the organ of the multiversal history that I have advocated here with the thesis that universal history is human only when it is neutralized and suspended by historicism: that is, when it becomes multiversal history.

I conclude by reminding you of the proposition with which I began: History, I said, is much too important a matter to be left to historians alone. I think that my philosophical remarks on universal history and multiversal history have made plausible not so much this proposition but rather (in a way that may, however, be useful in relation to the continuation of this lecture series) a very different and almost antithetical proposition—namely, that history is certainly much too important a matter to be left to philosophers alone.

Author's Notes

1. As was done with H. Plessner in the *Propyläen Weltgeschichte,* ed. G. Mann and A. Heuss, vol. 1 (1961), pp. 33–86. His essay, "Die Frage nach der

Conditio humana," is reprinted in his *Gesammelte Schriften*, ed. G. Dux, O. Marquard, and E. Ströker, vol. 8 (Frankfurt, 1983), pp. 136–217.

2. F. Schiller, *Sämtliche Werke*, centennial ed. in 16 vols., ed. E. von der Hellen et al. (Stuttgart, 1904–1905), vol. 13, pp. 3–24.

3. A. Borst, *Der Turmbau zu Babel. Geschichte der Meinungen über Ursprung und Vielfalt der Sprachen und Völker*, 4 vols. (Stuttgart, 1957–), vol. 1, p. 12.

4. E. Schulin, ed., *Universalgeschichte* (Cologne, 1974), esp. pp. 32–33.

5. F. W. J. Schelling, *Erster Entwurf eines Systems der Naturphilosophie* (1799), in *Sämtliche Werke* (Stuttgart, 1856–1861), part 1, vol. 3 (1858), esp. pp. 15ff. and 287ff.

6. W. Wieland, "Entwicklung," in O. Brunner, W. Conze, and R. Koselleck, eds., *Geschichtliche Grundbegriffe. Historisches Lexikon zur politischsozialen Sprache in Deutschland*, vol. 2 (Stuttgart, 1975), pp. 199–228.

7. J. Burckhardt, *Weltgeschichtliche Betrachtungen*, in *Gesammelte Werke* (Basel and Stuttgart, 1955–), vol. 4 (1970), pp. 116ff. Cf. R. Koselleck, *Futures Past: On the Semantics of Historical Time*, trans. K. Tribe (Cambridge, Mass., 1985); original: *Vergangene Zukunft. Zur Semantik geschichtlicher Zeiten* (Frankfurt, 1979).

8. W. Dilthey, "Die Typen der Weltanschauung und ihre Ausbildung in den metaphysischen Systemen" (1911), in *Gesammelte Werke* (Leipzig and Berlin, 1913–), vol. 8, ed. B. Groethuysen (1931), esp. pp. 80–81, 140ff., and many other places. Cf. O. Marquard, "Leben und leben lassen. Anthropologie und Hermeneutik bei Dilthey," in F. Rodi, ed., *Dilthey-Jahrbuch*, vol. 2 (Göttingen, 1984), pp. 128–39.

9. O. Marquard, "Zur Geschichte des philosophischen Begriffs 'Anthropologie' seit dem Ende des 18. Jahrhunderts" (1965), in *Schwierigkeiten mit der Geschichtsphilosophie* (Frankfurt, 1982), pp. 122–44.

10. Cf. W. Lepenies, *Das Ende der Naturgeschichte. Wandel kultureller Selbstverständlichkeiten in den Wissenschaften des 18. und 19. Jahrhunderts* (Frankfurt, 1978).

11. G. Dux, *Die Logik der Weltbilder. Seinsstrukturen im Wandel der Geschichte* (Frankfurt, 1982).

12. Cf. M. Heidegger, *Sein und Zeit* (Halle, 1927), esp. pp. 235ff.

13. This "Author's Introduction," translated by T. Parsons, is printed as the introduction to Weber's *The Protestant Ethic and the Spirit of Capitalism* (New York, 1958), p. 13. Original: *Gesammelte Aufsätze zur Religionssoziologie*, vol. 1 (7th printing, Tübingen, 1978), p. 1.

14. C. Lévi-Strauss, *Structural Anthropology*, trans. C. Jacobson and B. G. Schoepf (Garden City, N.Y. 1967), p. 332.

15. E. Nordhofen, "Ein vergnügter Skeptiker. Odo Marquard, *Abschied vom Prinzipiellen*," in *Frankfurter Allgemeine Zeitung*, no. 267 (November 17, 1981), Literaturbeilage, p. 11.

Translator's Notes

a. The "saddle period" (*Sattelzeit*) is R. Koselleck's term for the period around 1750 when the concept of a unitary world History originated and quickly became popular. See the author's note 1 to "The Age of Unworldliness?" (chapter 5).

b. *Naherwartung*, "immediate expectation," is a term used to describe messianic-eschatological expectations in their acute form.

c. The "long march through the institutions" (on the analogy, of course, of Mao's "long march") was a prospect discussed by members of the West German student movement in the early seventies.

d. The yellow *tricot* is worn by the leader in the annual French bicycle race, the "Tour de France."

e. The essay, "Über Prometheische Scham," constitutes the first section of Günther Anders's *Die Antiquiertheit des Menschen. Über die Seele im Zeitalter der zweiten industriellen Revolution* (Munich, 1956).

f. On the non-Popperian sense in which Marquard uses the term, "historicism," see translator's note b to "Skeptics" (chapter 1).

g. "Le choix que je suis": J.-P. Sartre, *L'Être at le néant* (Paris, 1953), p. 638. See section 3 of Marquard's "The Question: To What Question Is Hermeneutics the Answer?" in *Farewell to Matters of Principle,* translated by Robert M. Wallace (Oxford, 1988).

h. Greek: the animal that links up. See n. 33 to "The End of Fate?" in *Farewell to Matters of Principle.*

i. On "polymythical thinking," see "In Praise of Polytheism: On Monomythical and Polymythical Thinking," in *Farewell to Matters of Principle.*

= 5 =

The Age of Unworldliness?
A Contribution to
the Analysis of the Present

Our age has many names. It is supposed to be the age of "industrial society" or "late capitalism" or "scientific and technical civilization," or the "atomic age"; it is supposed to be the age of the "work society" or the "leisure society" or the "information society"; it is supposed to be the age of "functional differentiation," or the "epoch of epochal breaks," or the "postconventional age," or the "post-European age" (already), or simply "modernity" (or even "post-modernity" already)—and so on. This condition of having many names is an indirect form of anonymity: Our age and world find themselves in a crisis of orientation partly, it seems, because they are less and less sure which of these labels they should identify themselves with. I am not going to undertake the task of resolving this orientation crisis; instead, what I will do here is, in a salutary manner (whose salutariness I will explain only at the end), to intensify it, by bringing an additional characterization into play, as follows: Our age is (perhaps among other things) the age of unworldliness [*Weltfremd-heit*].[a] I would like to explain and give a little shape to this proposed characterization under the following five headings: Utopias and apocalypses; people no longer grow up; tachogenic unworldliness; the continuing need for negativity; and a plea for an appreciation of continuities.

71

Utopias and Apocalypses

Whatever else our age may be, it is certainly also the age of the rotating succession of utopias and apocalypses, of enthusiasm for a salvation in this world and certainty of impending catastrophes in it, of immediate expectation either of heaven on earth or of hell on earth, and, in any case, of superemphatic philosophies of progress and of downfall. Why do both of these form part of our world?

On the one hand we have the philosophies of progress and the utopias. A central element of our modern world, which has ultimately become industrial society and the society of work, is the idea of progress, the idea of mankind's self-improvement or even self-perfection: Everything gets better and better faster and faster, and may even soon, finally, really become good. This idea gains acceptance in the eighteenth century. At first—true to the "saddle period"[1] around 1750—it is formulated by the modern philosophy of history, of which the names of Turgot, Voltaire, Condorcet, Kant, Fichte, Hegel, and Marx can be taken as representative, and which can be understood as a secularization (according to Löwith) or a reoccupation (according to Blumenberg) of the pattern of salvation in the Christian theology of history: Through history, mankind pursues its salvation, the production of its good life. Then, after the disillusionment of emancipatory immediate expectation by (first of all) the French Revolution, the care of the idea of progress is taken over by positivist doctrines of stages and biological, psychoanalytic and sociological theories of evolution, of which the names of Schelling, Comte, Darwin, Spencer, Freud, Gehlen, Habermas, and Luhmann can be taken as representative. The quick march to salvation is replaced by the long march through the species and institutions; through history, mankind pursues the perfection of technique and the assurance of its survival. The basic pattern remains the same: The earlier is surpassed by the later, and the primitive by the developed, which is to say, concretely, the raw is surpassed by the cooked, nature by culture, the wild by the tamed, the pleasure principle by the reality principle, force by law, the clan by the state, myth by logos, accident by science, fate by technique, need by plenty, fantasy by observation, fiction by reality, illusion by critique, inequality by equality, repression by freedom, primeval man by late culture. In short, the earlier, which is underage and immature, is surpassed by the later, which is adult and mature, and by the latest, which is most adult and most mature. This perspective—which can be documented by the metaphors of the ages of man that are found in all theories of progress—implies that mankind is busily engaged in leaving its childhood behind it, and is thus making every effort to become continually more grown-up. The latest human beings are the most mature, the most grown-up human beings in the history of the world, and our age, as the product of the stripping off of its earlier immaturities and unworldlinesses, is the age of perfect adulthood. Seen in the perspective of salvation in this world, world history is the history of the progress of increasing grown-upness.

On the other hand we have the philosophies of decadence and downfall, and the apocalypses. An equally central element of our modern world, which has ultimately become industrial society and the society of work, is the idea of decadence and downfall, of mankind's self-destruction or even self-annihilation: Everything gets worse and worse faster and faster, and may even very soon, finally, really become fatal. The pattern of increasing maturity, which I sketched, is not disputed by this idea; rather, it continues to be upheld, precisely in those places where mankind's history of progress is perceived not as a history of gain but as a history of loss: as a history of the decadence and downfall produced by progress. This perception occurs, remarkably, at the same time as the positive career of the idea of progress and utopia in the philosophies of history and evolution. For the thesis that the growth of technology and of civilization is a loss and a process of decadence also comes into play—true to the "saddle period"—in the middle of the eighteenth century. Beginning in 1750, with his *Discourse on the Arts and Sciences,* Rousseau gave a proto-Green, negative answer to the question whether the progress of science and technology was good for man, and spoke in the name of nature against the history of progress. Since that time, this "no" has been repeated continually: in romanticism (by, for example, Novalis) at the beginning of the nineteenth century, and in Lebensphilosophie (by, for example, Nietzsche) at its end; and after Spengler, Klages, and Heidegger, the surge of the Greens is the current reprise of the interpretation of progress as decadence and downfall and of the supposed path to salvation as the path to catastrophe. There is nothing new under the sun, even if the latter is sometimes obscured by smog. As I said, the fundamental pattern, the pattern of increasing maturity, remains the same here, only now it is revalued, and where previously one rejoiced, now one quakes and complains; and where the principle of hope previously reigned, now it is the principle of fear. For we agree that mankind is busily engaged in leaving its childhood behind it, and is thus making every effort to become more grown-up: That is absolutely true. Only, it is bad. Our age, one in which great progress has been made in decadence or downfall, is the terrible era of hypertrophic grown-upness: It is the unlucky age of a great loss, namely, the loss of the childlikeness of human beings. For here, too, the rule is that the latest human beings are the most mature, the most grown-up human beings in the history of the world. Our age, as a product of the stripping off of its earlier capacities for direct experience and for creative fantasy, is the age of complete, or almost complete, grown-upness. Seen in the perspective of catastrophe, the history of the world is the history of the decline that the loss of childlikeness represents.

The expectation of liberation and fear of catastrophe, utopian philosophies of progress and apocalyptic philosophies of downfall—both of these belong to our modern world. Why both of them? I spoke of their rotating succession: They are "hostile brothers." It is not one of them but both that belong—essentially simultaneously, in their pendulum motion—to the modern world. Why both of them?

People No Longer Grow Up

I shall attempt to answer this question by, first of all, pointing to the following state of affairs: At about the same time as the simultaneous triumph of the philosophies of progress and the philosophies of downfall we also encounter—once again true to the "saddle period," and beginning in the eighteenth century—what has been called the "discovery of the child."[2] A child is not a small grown-up, but something different from a grown-up, namely, a child: This, Philippe Ariès has shown, is a modern discovery, made about three hundred years ago. Hardly two hundred years ago romanticism, impressed by Rousseau's doctrine of the good savage, sharpened this discovery of the child into the conviction that the child is the true human being, and that growing up (as the loss of childlikeness) is a falling-off from being human— that is, that growing up is, in the life of the individual, what the modern culture of progress itself is in the history of mankind: the story of the destruction of the true, "authentic," natural human being, the good savage who, in our alienated world, the child alone still is. Since then, children and youth are regarded as setting the authoritative standard for human beings. This opinion has found so many adherents that even schools sometimes urge their teachers to be only the pupils of their students. Growing up is the Fall. The only people who escape it, it seems, are those who refuse to grow up. Some think that means the artists; others think it means marginal groups and dropouts (from bohemia to alternative self-discovery groups); and the modern youth movements think it means, above all, children and youth themselves. It is not an accident that their garb today is the "savage look," the uniform of the good savage; for what we see passing by, bearded and shaggy, are not ungroomed human beings but well-groomed quotations from Rousseau. Part of this, on all sides, is the increased importance of the question, "How can I remain young?" and the flood of attempts to answer it satisfactorily: from sports to cosmetics to the development of the possibility of being a perpetual student. Because one nevertheless continues (if only for biological reasons) to grow older, the feeling comes into being that the modern grown-up world— as the world of the most grown-up grown-ups in the history of the world up to this point—restricts and stifles the world of children and youth. Present-day youth fights against this, and sometimes in an uncivilized way: For in the good savage, savage behavior of course demonstrates his goodness. The ultimate result of the excessive modern upward revaluation of childhood and youth, encouraged by the interpretation of progress as decadence and downfall, is that youth (with the applause of their elders) experiments with revolt—as a resistance movement against growing up. All of this is characteristic, to a large extent, of our present situation.

This situation of apparently expanding grown-upness and of the negative evaluation of it by our praise of the child and by youth protest needs, in my opinion, to be reexamined carefully. In doing this it is important, departing from previous analyses, to consider the following possibility: Perhaps it is not the case at all that modern grown-ups are *too grown-up* and *too unchildlike*. Perhaps, instead, the opposite is the case: that they are *not grown-up enough* and they are *too childlike*, and that, following the pattern of a "ressentiment," their praise of children is only praise of their own weakness: of the tendency of modern grown-ups to infantilism and childlike behavior, and of their incapacity for being grown-up—their proneness to unworldliness. And indeed, that will be my thesis in what follows: We do not lack childlikeness, rather, we have too much of it; for the rule, with human beings in the modern world, is that they no longer grow up, because this is the age of unworldliness. What I mean by saying that people no longer grow up is not what has no doubt always been the case, and what psychoanalysis has only reminded us of, impressively, once more: namely, to what a great extent, in everything that we do and think, we quote and remain the child that we once were—with relations to parents and siblings—and indeed we also and especially do this in the frequent, and frequently harmless, cases in which this does not lead to neurosis. "And then, the fundamental fact is that *there's no such thing as a grown-up person.*"[3] This is what a priest in the French Resistance, quoted at the beginning of Malraux's *Anti-Memoirs,* says about what he has learned from hearing confessions. I think that a confessor could have said the same thing a thousand years earlier; so it is something old, and thus nothing new. What is new is, rather, something else, which I will describe in the next section.

Tachogenic Unworldliness

What is new is a distinctive, specifically modern impairment of the process of growing up. I call it tachogenic unworldliness because it is a result of the accelerated speed (in Greek: *to táchos*) with which reality changes in modern times. In order to characterize it (which I cannot do fully, here), I would like to make five remarks.

The Obsolescence of Experience

The first characteristic feature of tachogenic unworldliness is the accelerated obsolescence of experience.[4] For barely a quarter of a millennium we have lived in a world, the modern world, in which more and more things change faster and faster. One of the distinctive characteristics of this world, as especially Reinhart Koselleck and Hermann Lübbe (following Jacob Burckhardt's interpretation of historical crises as "accelerated processes") have pointed out, is the acceleration of change. Where, for example, 2,000 years ago there was a forest, 1,000 years ago a field, and 500 years ago a house, 150 years ago there was a weaving mill, 75 years ago a train station, 25 years ago an airport, today there is a space satellite terminal, and what will be there ten years from now we do not know yet. The progress of science, technology, and worker productivity contributes to growth in the speed of innovation in almost all areas (and the exceptions are declining in number), which means at the same time that more and more things become obsolete faster and faster. This last observation also holds for our experience, because in our life-world the situations in which and for which we acquired our experience recur less and less frequently. Consequently, rather than becoming self-reliant, which is to say grown-up, through a continuous increase in our experience and our knowledge of the world, we more and more regularly fall back again into the situation of those for whom the world is predominantly unknown, new, alien, and enigmatic—that is, into the situation of children. Experience is the antidote, and probably the only antidote, for unworldliness; but now it no longer gets any grip. Since, nowadays, what is familiar becomes obsolete at a faster and faster rate, and the future world will increasingly be different from the world which we have experienced so far, the world becomes foreign to us (as modern human beings), and we become unworldly. Modern grown-ups become childlike. Even when we become gray, we remain green. People no longer grow up.

The Rise of Hearsay

The second characteristic feature of tachogenic unworldliness is the rapid rise of hearsay. As a result of the triumphal progress of the empirical sciences in modern times, there has never been a time when there were as many new experiences, as much new learning, as there is today. But we do not have these experiences ourselves; other people have them for us. Today even a specialist in empirical science, such as (for example) an experimental physicist, himself performs—if only for reasons of expense and time—at most 2 to 5 percent of the experiments on whose results he has to rely continually. In order to make innovation in experience possible (under conditions of acceleration), experience becomes superspecialized, dependent, for example, on specialized jargon and involving a lot of apparatus. Thus we increasingly have to accept experience that we have not had ourselves but are only acquainted with through hearsay—hearsay that is administered, to a large extent, by specialized, general-purpose, and sensational media, down to illustrated magazines like *Der Spiegel*. This means that the more scientifically experience, in our world, is accumulated, the more we have to have faith; and I emphasize this, because it sounds paradoxical: Precisely because experience, in modern times, is accumulated in a more and more scientific manner, we have to base our beliefs more and more on hearsay. This having to have faith—that is, dependence on experiences that one has not had, or has not yet had, oneself—was always the situation of children, and today, in the modern world, just this has become the normal situation of the grown-up, who thus, tachogenically unworldly, becomes, in a new way, a child. People no longer grow up.

The Expansion of Schooling

The third characteristic feature of tachogenic unworldliness is the expansion of schooling. Someone who—like modern man, whose own experiences more and more quickly become obsolete, and whose new, "specialist" experiences are predominantly not ones that he has himself—someone who no longer experiences things for himself has to cultivate substitutes for experience. Such a cultivation of substitutes for experience (of an experience-acquiring process that is relieved of and remote from experience, the process that people have in mind nowadays when they talk about "learning") is schooling, understood in the widest sense, so as to include kindergarten, higher education, continuing education, and education for senior citizens: schooling, which, for just this reason, first really comes into existence, and in any case first expands, in modern times, because, as a substitute for experience, more and more has to be learned. Thus school takes hold of more and more parts of the reality of our lives; and the unworldliness that school requires—because it trains people for adulthood under conditions of childhood, that is, through a moratorium on being grown-up—devolves, little by little, onto reality. Only initially is it an exaggeration to which teachers and educational policy makers who never left school are inclined, when they designate school itself as life: Just as reality was once identified (from Schelling, through Wagner to surrealism) with art, such that seriousness was only "played" in the "total work of art," so reality now is identified with school, through the "total school." But the more (as a result of the tachogenic deficit of direct experience) one has to spend one's life experiencing—which is to say learning—indirectly, the more reality is literally on the point of really becoming a school. Man becomes, tendentially, nothing but a student, and thus every adult becomes, tendentially, the child that is hidden in every student, however old he may be. People no longer grow up.

The Boom in Fiction

The fourth characteristic feature of tachogenic unworldliness is the boom in (in the widest sense) "fiction."[6] When the world, because of the acceleration of change, becomes continually more complex, it increasingly needs what Luhmann calls "reductions of complexity," each of which involves quasi fictions: Every simplification of the world contains a vital lie. An exemplary finding is the following: Actions, and especially interactions having a significant order of magnitude, always take time. While this time is passing, and under conditions of acceleration, the orienting data on the basis of which the actions were undertaken change. From a certain temporal "point of no return" onward, the perspective inherent in the action requires one to ignore the changes in these data. Without this fiction of constancy one would never complete an action. When everything is in flux, every action that is carried through exacts such fictions; and it has to be said, against

Comte, that it is not the religious stage but the "positive" one that is characterized by its use of fiction. Of course, this leads precisely to an increase in the risk of unwanted side effects, so that large-scale plans, in particular, easily become "self-destroying prophecies." So we need a confidence that resists being undermined by this kind of experience. If necessary, the guarantees of this confidence are invented—for example (since Kant), in the form of postulates of practical reason.

Today these fictions are, as a rule, no longer absolute postulates, no longer the postulate of a superhuman omnipotence (God) that sets things straight again, or that of a transfinite patience in waiting for the results of this intervention (immortality). Instead, all fictions of constancy (such as are announced, in exemplary fashion, by the current inflationary use of the formula, "I take it as a given that. . . ," which is a formula for a fiction of constancy) are confidence-guaranteeing postulates, for example, as ceteris-paribus clauses. These, in their turn, constitute an increasingly complicated ensemble, which needs experts to look after it. That is why, today, we no longer postulate postulates; instead we postulate, and we pay, postulators: the industry of orientation-data-production, with its special department for fiction-confection, which includes not only the computer forecasting statisticians (and among them, the constructors of world models), but also the professional dreamers. Here, in each case, the overwhelming majority of those who take part in the action (and that includes all of us) is no longer really in a position to pass judgment on the degree to which the data reflect reality: The difference between the perception of reality and fiction becomes blurred. A central fact about the present seems to me to be that both of these—the perception of reality, and fiction—increasingly take on a semifictive character, and thus tend to converge with each other. That is why it is so easy, nowadays, to ignore really terrible things and to be convinced by imagined positive things, and almost easier, even, to believe in imagined terrible things and to be blind to really positive ones— in other words, to accept what suits one and to suppress what does not. Thus tachogenic unworldliness creates a disposition toward illusions, by which people, engaged in dreams, become childlike. People no longer grow up.

Our Willingness to Accept Illusion

That is why the fifth characteristic feature of tachogenic unworldliness is our increasing willingness to accept illusion. It is a product of what Joachim Ritter called the "disharmony between what we come from and what is to come," and what Reinhardt Koselleck calls the growing "split" between "experience and expectation,"[7] which is produced by the increasing acceleration of change: Less and less past experience will also be future experience, so that it is less possible to gauge one's expectation of what is to come by one's experience up to the present. So expectations, no longer being congruent with and controlled by experience, become boundless and, in their tendency, illusionary; and when the philosophy of history, by dismissing the topos of "historia magistra vitae,"[b] rejects the authority of what is old, and the society that is oriented toward claims rejects the authority of what experience has shown to be possible, it is easy for this necessity—the necessary loss of the guidance of experience—to be pronounced a virtue. Then what happens is a flight from the *loss* of experience into a *renunciation* of experience—into, for example, the great boom in a priori theories and salvation plans. But above all, people become anticipators without experience, which is to say, dreamers.

What one expects then is just what one can no longer experience, which is familiarity or "at-homeness." The more this familiarity is no longer experienced, the more it is—impatiently—anticipated, through the illusion of a ("this-worldly") world that is finally no longer alien, but whole, restored. Precisely this world then becomes a direct hope, a direct claim. Children, for whom reality is overwhelmingly alien, need, to offset this, an iron ration of something familiar: their teddy bear, which they drag along with them everywhere for just this purpose. In just the same way, modern grown-ups—for whom the world again, tachogenically, becomes permanently alien—need the ideological immediate expectation of a whole, restored world: It is the mental teddy bear of the modern, once again childlike, grown-up. For a world in which less and less of what was will still be there in the future—in which, then, tachogenically, less and less of what we come from will be what is to come—such a world is stamped by the loss of continuity. That loss enthrones the illusion by which people are made childlike. People do not grow up any more.

All of this helps the modern world to become what I called the age of unworldliness.

The Continuing Need for Negativity

Now, in my opinion it is this tachogenic unworldliness that leads, in the modern world, to the rotating succession (which I outlined in the beginning) between utopias and apocalypses, positive and negative illusions— or pipe dreams and nightmares. This rotation promotes what is discussed nowadays under the rubric of "value change," but which is no such thing, since the phenomenon in question is from the beginning only an oscillation between pretended values—that is, the modern rotating succession of utopias and apocalypses. At the moment it is the turn, again, of apocalypse: of the nightmare. For another peculiarity of the age of tachogenic unworldliness is, apparently, this: it is not only positive expectations—claims and hopes—that become illusionary, but also negative expectations, fears. Because expectations in general become unworldly, disappointments of positive expectations no longer lead to sober disillusionment, but to a sort of negative drunkenness: The upsetting of excessive hopes no longer yields an appreciation of reality, but instead yields panic. Evidence of this can be seen, I think, in the current tendency to assign a negative value to the culture of progress.

For we should really be living in the age of sober disillusionments. Cultural progress, especially in technology, used to produce great benefits at small expense, and now—when much that makes life easier has been achieved—produces at greater expense and with greater negative effects on the environment what are now only relatively smaller benefits. But if smaller and smaller benefits require and are paid for with larger and larger detriments, we finally arrive at a zero balance between expense and effect; and beyond this limit of utility the marginal utility of progress becomes negative. That may currently be the situation in some areas (though certainly not in all): I—who may count as a neutral observer since I myself cannot drive an automobile, so that my comments are only those of a passenger—could imagine, for example, that the expansion of transportation by automobile in our country might in the long run produce more nuisances than satisfactions. But first, since the advocate of change has the burden of proof, that would have to be made plausible, by taking into account not only the manifest but also the latent functions of the automobile system (including, for example, the fact that by their encapsulating effect, autos seems to meet the need for solitude under conditions of "massification"). And, second, the remedy then would not lie in increasing the level of lamentation and in the inflationary convening of tribunals of neoethicists, but rather in the pragmatic search for an optimal proportion of nuisances to satisfactions, enforcing birth control for automobiles only as a last resort. The reasonable way to behave here is this: gratefully to enjoy the benefits that have been obtained, and, when this proves to be necessary, to forgo unrestricted further expansion in certain matters, prudently and without complaint, and in a climate of sober, balanced consideration. However, we do not live in a climate of sober, balanced consideration, but in a climate of hysterical fear; for wherever one looks, refined panic reigns. Why in the world should that be the case?

The cultural accomplishments that relieve human beings of burdens seem to pass through three stages: At first they are welcomed; then they are taken for granted; and finally they are cast in the role of enemy. The behavior of human beings parallels this process: At first they work assiduously to construct these disencumbering accomplishments; then they casually consume what they have achieved; and finally they become afraid of it, and attack it. The last stage presupposes the second, and the second in turn presupposes the first; and what this means (if I see the matter correctly) is that the later attack on culture's disencumbering accomplishments comes about not in spite of, but precisely on account of their success; or, to put if differently, it is precisely relief from what is negative[8] that disposes us to assign a negative value to what provides the relief. To explain what I mean by this abstract formula I will first of all provide three examples. The more illnesses medicine conquers, the stronger becomes the inclination to declare medicine itself to be an illness. The more benefits mankind derives from chemistry, the more chemistry comes to be suspected of having been invented solely to poison mankind. An finally, the longer wars are avoided, the more thoughtlessly the existing measures to provide for peace are regarded as pure belligerence. In short: Relief from negative circumstances itself creates a disposition to assign a negative character to the agency of relief, and liberation from threats itself makes the liberating agency appear threatening.

This nexus, which initially seems entirely paradoxical, becomes plausible if we assume the existence of a certain constancy or (more accurately) slowness to change that characterizes the human need for negativity. Human beings' susceptibility to fear leads them to expect, more or less permanently, a certain quantity of adversity. For human beings—by nature creatures of deficiency,[c] who are forced to become cultural creatures in order to compensate for their natural deficiencies—confront a rich array of adversities, in the form of natural enemies and savageries in nature, frailties in their own condition, illnesses, the trouble and the burden of physical labor, the disorders of life with other human beings, the renunciation of aggression, which cultural progress imposes on them, and so on. In order to turn these adversities into something useful for life, humans have to be ready to deal with negative things, so it makes sense that matters are arranged as I described them, that human beings' susceptibility to fear leads them to expect, more or less permanently, a certain quantity of adversity. To that extent adverse (that is, negative) things are—even as an opportunity to overcome something—a kind of anthropological possession from which humans find it difficult to separate, especially when they have to do so rapidly and without having anything to put in their place, because humans are conservative creatures, who are reluctant to renounce anything, even if it is something unpleasant. That is why it comes about, when adversities are permanently dismantled by cultural development, not only that this quickly ceases to be honored as a benefit (and is taken for granted, instead), but also, and above all, that we embark (mostly unconsciously) on the great search for a substitute for the lost adversities—for negativities to compensate for the shortage of negativities—or for menaces to take the place of the menaces that have been overcome; and this search is intensified when, as is largely the case in our country at present,

risks that are pregnant with negativity can no longer be found in sufficient quantity even on "adventure vacations." Thus the adversities that
human cultural labors have increasingly dispelled from reality, and
whose absence (as habits that are as difficult to renounce as addictions)
now causes withdrawal symptoms, are in the end increasingly sought
and (actually or imaginatively) "found" in the very cultural labor that
spares us the adversities. If culture conquers more and more threats,
culture itself, as a substitute menace, is nominated as the new threat,
which one thinks that one has to conquer (say, by an alternative life-
style). Or, putting it differently, and more abstractly: It is precisely relief
from what is negative that disposes us to assign a negative character to
the agency of relief. This is because—and this is one of the great sources
of fear in our time—people fear above all what spares them fears, just
because it spares them fears; and because the fear, having lost its job in
reality, goes in search of opportunities to have it, and finds them, too, at
almost any cost: ultimately, in developed culture itself. The more the
modern world eradicates earlier frightful things, the more it is itself now
blamed for frightful things, which, if need be (because not enough of
them are to be found here at home), are recruited through fright-
confirming tourism. The more successfully technology functions to
make life easier, the less restraint we feel in experiencing it as making life
more difficult; and the more it in fact enables us to protect the environment, the more it is declared to encumber the environment. And analogously, the more effectively capitalism produces welfare, the more energetically it is indicted as ill-fare; the more the market solves problems,
the more it itself seems to be a problem; and it is only because socialist
planned economies solve these problems less well that people are more
indulgent toward them. The more reliably the state prevents civil wars,
the more recklessly it is itself regarded as grounds for civil war; the more
parliamentary democracy spares people repression, the more easily it is
itself proclaimed to be repressive; and the more law replaces violence,
the more law itself is finally regarded as (if need be, "structural") violence. In short, the more culture makes reality no longer an antagonist,
the more culture itself is regarded as the antagonist. In this great inver-
sion of the negative, what is at work is a sort of ill-fare nostalgia of the
welfare world, which is more easily accused of disadvantages, the more

disadvantages it eliminates, and toward which (in defense of one's possessions) one becomes the more fearful, the more reasons for fear it removes. Thus the rule is, in fact, that it is precisely liberation from what is adverse that makes the agency of liberation adverse; or, abstractly, it is precisely relief from what is negative that disposes us to assign a negative character to the agency of relief.

What this formula expresses could be called the conservation law of the need for negativity. But it is not, I hope, really a law, nor is it even a rule of thumb that folk tradition overlooked. Instead, my thesis here is that the nexus that I have formulated—according to which, when one is spared something negative, one seeks it (because from then on one misses it) in precisely that which spares one from it—that this nexus operates only when humans, tachogenically, become all too unworldly, and when their inhibition against being adult (that is, their acceleration-contingent infantilization rate) exceeds a certain level, which, admittedly, it not uncommonly does nowadays. Then, and only then, I think, does this nexus take hold and operate; but when it does so, its effects are ruinous. It is because I want to warn against this nexus that I draw attention to it. I want to warn against this temptation to invert what is negative, and against being prompted by relief from what is negative to assign a negative character to the agency of relief. It is for this reason that I warn against too much tachogenic unworldliness and against too much acceleration-contingent infantilization; and for the same reason I recommend more courage to be adult.

A Plea for an Appreciation of Continuities

This warning and this encouragement have no prospects of success if the modern world is *only* what I have so far described it as: only the age of unworldliness. My opinion, which was signaled by the question mark in the title of my lecture, is this: It is true that the modern world is also the age of unworldliness, but that is not all that it is. Granted, we are exposed to modern existence's increasing velocity of change and of obsolescence, which is precisely what makes us tachogenically unworldly, by virtue of the fact that (on account of the acceleration of change) less and less of what we come from will still be what is to come. It is, after all, precisely this increasing discontinuity between what we come from and what is to come that robs experience of its power and gives power to illusion, including, in particular, negative illusions. But at the same time, as compensation, there are decelerations: The age of unworldliness is at the same time the age of compensatory continuities. It is vitally important for us to pay affirmative attention precisely to these compensatory continuities—that is, to develop and to cultivate an appreciation of continuities. In conclusion, but without any claim to comprehensiveness, I will point out here only three forms of this appreciation of continuities.

We need *a sense of history*.[9] We do not have to begin by inventing it, because it exists in our world, and indeed in abundance. The fact that, in modern times, less and less of what we come from will be what is to come is compensated by the art of taking more and more of what we come from along with us into what is to come, by means of the faculty of history, a faculty that—as a sort of substitute adulthood for tachogenic un-grown-ups—first arose in modern times to compensate for the modern acceleration of obsolescence. No age has obliterated more of the past than ours has, and at the same time no age has held fast to more of the past: storing it in museums, conserving it carefully, protecting it ecologically, collecting it archivally, reconstructing it archaeologically, remembering it historiographically. Our modern tachogenic continuing destruction of the past is compensated by our modern historically minded continuing preservation of the past. Without it, we would no longer be able (in this age of breaks in continuity) to meet our need for continuity, or (in this age of unworldliness) to meet our need for familiarity and to endure the changes in reality. For the less continuity our sense of history provides, the more flight into illusion we will engage in. In relation to the latter, the sense of history has a disillusioning, sobering effect. We could not live without a sense of history.

We also need *an appreciation of usages*.[10] We do not need to begin by inventing them, either, because they are there (the only difference in the modern age being that there is a more variegated mixture of them in any one place than there used to be). As "moeurs," customs, usual practices, and traditions, they become indispensable precisely in modern times; for the more everything continually changes (in this age of tachogenic unworldliness), the more one needs life routines that are governed by usages—what one does because it has always been done that way. The more difficult the life-situation, the greater the need for routine. These normal practices (which in some cases are traditions belonging to rational subsystems) also belong in the category of compensatory continuities, and it has to be admitted that we cannot get along without them. Thus people need help in developing an appreciation of the usual; because usual practices are becoming more and more important, as compensations for acceleration, and I suspect that they are more and more powerfully present. For without them we would no longer be able (in this age of breaks in continuity) to meet our need for continuity, or (in this age of unworldliness) to meet our need for familiarity and to endure the changes in reality. For the less continuity our usages provide, the more flight into illusion we will engage in. In relation to the latter, usages (that is, traditions) have a disillusioning, sobering effect. We could not live without usages.

We also need *to hold fast to enlightenment*.[11] It is the modern tradition that—as the will to adulthood [*Mündigkeit*], to being grown-up—turns the courage to be sober into a routine. Because one should not deviate from usages unnecessarily, neither should one deviate unnecessarily from this tradition, from the usage that is modernity. Here one has to rescue enlightenment from those who want to transform its function into that of a performance-enhancing "dope" for revolutionaries. For, at least in my opinion (as one whose skeptical traditionalism takes the form of a traditionalism of modernity), it is not enlightenment, but an illusion, to expect to alleviate the negative effects of the modern acceleration of change by means of a greater acceleration (and to alleviate its unworldliness by greater unworldlinesses): by making antimodernism futuristic through the revolutionary urge to move beyond modernity. For that, in my view, would also mean to move beyond enlightenment—the enlightenment that, as must be stated clearly, is a bourgeois tradition to which, for the sake of sobriety, one has to hold fast by doing something that today is thoroughly unpopular: acquiescing in one's own bourgeois-ness.

Allow me to make one brief concluding observation. The label, "the age of unworldliness" (just like the label, "the age of compensatory continuities") comes into play in a supplementary role: as an additional name for an age that, as I said initially, already has many names and is caught in a crisis of orientation because, for one thing, it is less and less sure with which of these labels it has to identify itself. My intention here, as I said in the beginning, was not to set this orientational havoc to rights. Rather, as I also said, it was to intensify the confusion in a salutary way: by increasing the multiplicity of names for our age. Why is this multiplicity of names salutary? It seems to me that as the number of controversial labels for the present increases (in accordance with the maxim: divide and think!), the danger of mono-diagnostic one-sided views declines and the individual's diagnostic freedom increases. This is what is important to the skeptic (such as myself), because skepticism is, after all, an appreciation of the division or separation of powers, including even the powers that names are. In this sense I have not characterized, but only cocharacterized our age, in naming it (with a question mark) the age of unworldliness.

Author's Notes

1. The concept of the "saddle period" refers to the period of European history circa and shortly after 1750. It was coined by R. Koselleck in his "Richtlinien für das Lexikon politisch-sozialer Begriffe in der Neuzeit," *Archiv für Begriffsgeschichte* 9 (1967), pp. 82, 91, 95. Cf. Koselleck's introduction to O. Brunner, W. Conze, R. Koselleck, eds., *Geschichtliche Grundbegriffe. Historisches Lexikon zur politisch-sozialen Sprache in Deutschland*, vol. 1 (Stuttgart, 1972), esp. p. XV.

2. Philippe Ariès, *L'enfant et la vie familale sous l'Ancien Régime* (Paris, 1960); translated by R. Baldick as *Centuries of Childhood* (New York, 1962).

3. A. Malraux, *Anti-Memoirs,* trans. T. Kilmartin (New York, 1968), p. 1; the original work is *Antimémoires* (Paris, 1967).

4. Cf. H. Lübbe, "Erfahrungsverluste und Kompensationen. Zum philosophischen Problem der Erfahrung in der gegenwärtigen Welt," *Giessener Universitätsblätter* 12.2 (1979): 42–53.

5. Cf. J. Burckhardt, *Weltgeschichtliche Betrachtungen,* in *Gesammelte Werke* (Basel and Stuttgart, 1955–), vol. 4 (1970), p. 116; R. Koselleck, *Vergangene Zukunft. Zur Semantik geschichtlicher Zeiten* (Frankfurt, 1979), translated by K. Tribe as *Futures Past: On the Semantics of Historical Time* (Cambridge, Mass. 1985); and H. Lübbe, *Zukunft ohne Verheissung? Sozialer Wandel als Orientierungsproblem* (Zurich, 1976).
6. Cf. O. Marquard, "Kunst als Antifiktion. Über den Weg der Wirklichkeit ins Fiktive," in D. Henrich, W. Iser, eds., *Funktionen des Fiktiven,* Poetik und Hermeneutik 10 (Munich, 1983); and O. Marquard, *Krise der Erwartung— Stunde der Erfahrung. Zur ästhetischen Kompensation des modernen Erfahrungsverlustes* (Konstanz, 1982).
7. Cf. J. Ritter, *Subjektivität. Sechs Aufsätze* (Frankfurt, 1974), p. 27 and many other places; R. Koselleck, article, "Geschichte/Historie," in *Geschichtliche Grundbegriffe* (see n. 1), vol. 2 (Stuttgart, 1975), esp. pp. 658ff.
8. On "relief [*Entlastung,* "unburdening"] from what is negative," see A. Gehlen, *Anthropologische Forschung* (Reinbek bei Hamburg, 1961), pp. 64ff.
9. Cf. Ritter, *Subjektivität,* esp. pp. 105ff.
10. Cf. O. Marquard, 'Die Erziehung des Menschengeschlechts—eine Bilanz," in *Der Traum der Vernunft. Vom Elend der Aufklärung. Eine Veranstaltungsreihe der Akademie der Künste, Berlin,* 1st ser. (Darmstadt and Neuwied, 1985), pp. 125–33.

Translator's Notes

a. "Unworldliness" is, I believe, the least unsatisfactory brief translation of *Weltfremdheit.* What is meant is not the *other*-worldliness of religious "unworldliness," but merely the common, everyday variety that we also describe as innocence, naiveté, unfamiliarity with the "ways" of the world.
b. *Historia magistra vitae*—"history is the teacher of life"—summed up the classical view that the "lessons" of, say, Roman history, could be applied to one's own historical situation because human affairs had certain basic patterns that simply repeated themselves. This conflicts, on the face of it, with the idea of progress. Koselleck discusses the demise of this classical view in a chapter of the book cited in the author's note 5 to this essay.
c. The characterization of human beings as *Mängelwesen,* "creatures of deficiency," was popularized by Arnold Gehlen's *Der Mensch* (see translator's note a to "Unburdenings," in chapter 2).

=6=

On the Unavoidability
of the Human Sciences

One of the many anecdotes about the great Danish physicist, Niels Bohr, goes as follows. Bohr receives a visitor at his ski lodge. The visitor notices a horseshoe that is fastened above the door of the lodge. Surprised, he asks Bohr, "Do you, as a natural scientist, believe in that?" To which Bohr replies, "Of course I don't believe in it. But I have been assured that horseshoes work even if one doesn't believe in them."

In my opinion, there is a similarity between the relationship that most people now have to the human sciences [*Geisteswissenschaften*] and Bohr's relationship, which he characterized in a subtle and insurpassably philosophical manner, to the horseshoe. The similarity is that although people do not believe in the human sciences, they rely on them, because—as it seems to me—they simply have nothing else left to rely on. Of course at the same time there are also some profound differences between the horseshoe and the human sciences, among them being these two: The institution of the horseshoe is old, whereas the institution of the human sciences is new; and the human sciences, in contrast to the horseshoe, are (more or less) irreplaceable. I would like to underscore this by advocating, in my reflections here, the following fundamental thesis: The more modern the modern world becomes, the more unavoidable the human sciences become. I plead for taking this fact into account in every way, from esteem through financial support. My plea, in this regard, contains the following four sections: contradiction of a prejudgment; the compensatory role of the human sciences; in praise of ambiguity; and new prospects for anthropology?

Contradiction of a Prejudgment

The prejudgment that I would like to contradict here is widespread even today, and runs as follows: The human sciences are increasingly made obsolete by the modernization of our world, because part of the modern world is the birth and expansion of the hard sciences, the experimental ones (that is, above all, the natural sciences, but also the quantitative social sciences), which increasingly render superfluous the sciences that are not, or are not yet, experimental, which is to say, the narrative sciences—the *Geisteswissenschaften*. In other words, the long-run tendency in the modern world, and a product of the process of modernization, is for the human sciences to die off.

This prejudgment derives its vigor from the following historical assumption: First we had the human sciences, which were thus the "old sciences," and then the experimental natural sciences, as the "new sciences," came along. But this historical assumption is mistaken. My teacher of philosophy, Joachim Ritter (who died in 1974), drew attention to this fact—in a pointed way that is still worth reflecting on—in an address that he gave in 1961 on "The Task of the Human Sciences in Modern Society."[1] What he made clear is that the actual relationship is just the reverse: First we had the experimental natural sciences, and then the human sciences came along. The human sciences are younger than the natural sciences.

What I am giving here is not a lecture on the history of science, so I will document this statement only by a brief indication of the average time delay between the practical establishment of the experimental natural sciences and that of the human sciences, which is, initially, about a hundred (or something more than a hundred) years. This is already evident, symptomatically, in the interval of time that separates the two programmatic philosophical treatises, the one that aims at the natural sciences and the one that aims at the human sciences: Descartes's

Discours de la méthode [Discourse on Method] appears in 1637 and Vico's *Prinzipi di una scienza nuova* [Principles of a New Science] appears in 1725. This interval is then repeated between the two classical philosophical treatises on the foundations of these sciences: Kant analyzes the foundations of the natural sciences in 1781 in his *Critique of Pure Reason* and Dilthey analyzes the foundations of the human sciences in 1883 in his *Introduction to the Human Sciences* and his other contributions to the "critique of historical reason." The names of the two groups of sciences surface at a (symptomatically) similar interval: The term "natural sciences" [*Naturwissenschaften*] is common beginning in 1703, and the term "human sciences" [*Geisteswissenschaften*] is common beginning around 1847 or 1849. But all of this merely reflects the interval between the practical establishment of the respective sciences themselves. The decisive period of the breakthrough of the natural sciences (beginning with physics and chemistry) to exactitude—one thinks of Galileo, Torricelli, Boyle, Newton, Lavoisier, and so on—was the seventeenth and eighteenth centuries, whereas the decisive period of the breakthrough of the human sciences (the "contemplative," as opposed to the "pragmatic" human sciences,[2] that is, initially, the study of classical antiquity and then those of history, language, literature, and art) to their own paths—one thinks of Winckelmann, Heyne, Herder, Grimm, Bopp, Niebuhr, Ranke, Droysen, Burckhardt, and so on—was the eighteenth and nineteenth centuries. So the actual relationship is that, in modern times, it was the hard, natural sciences that first began their successful progress, and only then, after an initial delay of about one hundred years, did the human sciences emerge (with their institutionalization in the universities being concentrated in the second half of the nineteenth century).

Now, to pick up the question that Joachim Ritter asks after establishing this elementary state of affairs: What does this mean? Surely this: If the human sciences come into existence "after" the experimental sciences, it cannot be correct to say that they are made superfluous "by" the experimental sciences. Instead, since it is natural to interpret the "post" ["after"] as "propter" ["on account of"], the more plausible relationship is that both groups of sciences, together, are necessary and characteristic parts of the modern world, and specifically in such a

way (and this explains temporal delay) that the formation and development of the human sciences is an answer to the formation and development of the hard natural sciences. The experimental natural sciences
are the "challenge"; the human sciences are the "response."[a] In relation to the human sciences, the genesis of the experimental sciences is
not the cause of death but the cause of birth; or in other words, the
human sciences are not modernization's sacrificial victim but its result,
and are thus, themselves, insurpassably modern. Taking this conjec-
tural causal relationship as my point of departure, I will risk the following prognosis: Every future advance in the hard sciences—in the natural sciences and their transposition into technology, but also in the
experimental sciences of man—will enforce (with shorter and shorter
delays) an increasingly expanded need for human sciences. Or indeed,
putting it differently: The more modern the modern world becomes,
the more unavoidable the human sciences become.

Before I try to say something about why that is the case, I would like
to draw attention to the crucial conclusion that has to be drawn if I am
correct. We will have to say farewell to the great prognoses of the
atrophy or shrinkage of the human sciences, including the current
flood of lamentation about their present condition. This does not
absolve us of the duty to take seriously the transitory damages that
these sciences have suffered, which in Germany run from their loss of
substance due to emigration in the thirties (whose effects are still being
felt), through their mistaken orientation toward the tasks of training
teachers on a low level, and the shadow cast on their virtues in the
areas of memory and narrative by their transient affairs with mathe-
matics and ideology, to (finally) the problem of failures where their
institutionalization has been excessively specialized. But I do not see a
fundamental crisis of performance on the part of the human sciences.
Cassandra-like pronouncements are out of place. In many cases complaints are misconceived; for example, the fact that in comparison to
the nineteenth century and the beginning of this century, the share of
German human scientists in the world's gross product of human-
scientific genius has fallen, is in reality a success. The human sciences
themselves have in the meantime, as a result of the global processes of
modernization, become such a worldwide success, that in the world as

a whole there are more and more working human scientists, with the result that the relative share of the Germans naturally declines. The fact that they no longer discover most of what is discovered, but only some of it, is perfectly normal. Nevertheless, there *is* at present a crisis of the human sciences. But, if I see matters correctly, this crisis is due not to the fact that the supply of achievement in the human sciences is declining, but rather to the fact that the demand for human sciences— as a consequence of more and more rapid modernization processes— grows more rapidly than the productive capacity of the human sciences. To put it in a nutshell, the current crisis of the human sciences is not a "crisis of production" but a "crisis of excessive demand."[3] It is not, then, that the human sciences are dying off, but only that, although they are growing, they cannot keep pace with their modern unavoidability. This, however, does not conflict with, but supports my fundamental thesis: The more modern the modern world becomes, the more unavoidable the human sciences become.

The Compensatory Role of the Human Sciences

But why is that so, and how are we to understand it—that the modernization of our world, which is driven by the hard sciences, not only does not make the human sciences superfluous but is what first makes them necessary, and indeed more and more so? My answer—and here, for the time being, I continue to follow chiefly in the footsteps of Joachim Ritter—is this: The modernization that is driven by the experimental sciences causes losses on the level of the life-world, losses for which the human sciences help to compensate.[4] Allow me to recount the basic course of this process a little more concretely, by making three observations.

Neutralization

Someone who wants to carry out experiments that can be double-checked must make the experimenters interchangeable. But the experimenters are human beings, and human beings just are not easily interchangeable—not because they persist in containing (as marginal phenomena) subjective emotions that, operating (as it were) as regretta-

ble disturbing factors, adulterate the results, but because human beings are, in fact, primarily different, in the sense that (even apart from
their individuality) they are involved in different linguistic, religious,
cultural, and familial traditions, and they could not live at all if that
were not the case. For we human beings are always more our traditions than our experiments. Hence it is necessary first of all to use art
to make these human beings capable of engaging in experimentation—
which is just what is done in the modern experimental sciences, where
method requires each experimenter to relinquish his or her special
characteristics. "Methodical doubt" "neutralizes" (strictly in the technical, six-day bicycle-racing sense of that term) the historical worlds
that the experimenting scientists come from—for example, their religious traditions (that they are Buddhists, Moslems, Jews, Christians,
whether Protestant or Catholic, and so on). As long as the race is
"experimental," nothing is decided in terms of the worlds (for example, religious worlds) one comes from: and vice versa. But this neutralization of the worlds that people come from is successful only in the
laboratory, and not in life; and since there are people for whom the
laboratory is part of life, it is not even consistently successful there,
where, after all, people continually use traditional languages as well,
so as—by means of metaphors—to adopt scientific results to the brevity of human life. Thus, for example, talk of the "genetic code" is a
metaphor from the traditional field of images grouped around the
"book of nature," which itself is part of the field of images associated
with the "book of books," that is, the Bible.[5] But the fundamental rule
is that the modern sciences become exact—that is, they become experimental sciences—by neutralizing the life-world traditions in which
their scientists are situated, which is to say, by methodically relinquish-
ing the historical worlds they come from.

Homogeneity

This methodical renunciation of the historical worlds we come from
becomes the danger of their actual loss, as a consequence of modernizations. Modernizations consist in the—partial—replacement of the
worlds we come from with experimentally tested and technically generated object worlds [Sachwelten], which then require man, so that he

can get along in them, to be interchangeable, at the expense of his traditional heterogeneities. Man now becomes, in his life-world as well, an "expert" [*Sachverständiger*]; and what is becomes an "object" [*Sache*]: a subject for exact experiment, a technical instrument, an industrial product, an economically calculable commodity. And in the process, all of this, because it presses toward globalization, renders life-worlds uniform around the world. In a word: Homogeneity triumphs. As Hermann Lübbe, especially, has maintained (thus impressively extending Joachim Ritter's thesis),[6] this process accelerates: In the modern world, more and more things are more and more rapidly "objectified." That means that less and less of where people have come from seems to be able to remain what is to come; the worlds that people come from, historically, are increasingly in danger of obsolescence. But in the absence of compensation, that would be a loss that human beings could not endure, because increasingly the human need to inhabit a life-world that is colorful, familiar, and meaningful would not be met.

Compensation

So this loss cries out for compensation; and the aids in that compensation are the human sciences, which therefore come into existence precisely now—in modern times. Of course, if in the modern world all traditions, or even only most of them, were worn out, all help would arrive too late. We should not bewail this total crisis into existence: We are not so well off that we can afford that kind of indulgence in negativization and pride in our crises, which are attitudes that are after all contradicted every day by reality, with the abundance of intact traditions that it exhibits. In modern times too, and in modern times in particular, we humans are and remain always more our traditions than our modernizations. The human sciences help those traditions so that humans can endure these modernizations. Thus the human sciences are not (and I emphasize this in my capacity, which goes with my skepticism, as a traditionalist of modernity) opposed to modernization. Instead, insofar as they serve to compensate the damage done by modernization they in fact make modernization possible. To do this they need the art of making familiar, once again, worlds from which we come that are becoming alien. That is the hermeneutic art, interpretation. What one does with this art, when confronted with something that has become alien, is, as a rule, to look for a familiar set of concerns with which it would fit; and this set of concerns almost always constitutes a story. For human beings *are* their stories.[7] But stories have to be told. This is what the human sciences do: They compensate for the damage done by modernization by telling stories. And the more things are objectified, the more, in compensation, stories have to be told: Otherwise humans die of narrative atrophy. This underscores and makes more precise my fundamental thesis, that the more modern the modern world becomes, the more unavoidable the human sciences become, namely, as narrative sciences. They tell three types of stories, in particular.

Sensitizing Stories. Here the issue—in terms of compensation for the world's increasing colorlessness—is the need for a life-world that has color. Modernization has the effect of "disenchantment" (Max Weber), and this modern disenchantment of the world is compensated, also in modern times, by the substitute enchantment of the aesthetic realm (previously, there was never such a thing as autonomous, aesthetic art). That is why we see the specifically modern emergence of aesthetic appreciation, which is aided in its task of comprehension by the human sciences when they tell sensitizing stories.

Preserving Stories. Here the issue—in terms of compensation for the world's increasing alienness—is the need for a life-world that is familiar. Modernization has the effect of an accelerated artificialization (that is, denaturalization) and objectivization (that is, dehistoricization) of reality, both of which are compensated, in specifically modern fashion, by the development of an appreciation of nature (from the discovery of landscape to nature conservation) and by the development of an appreciation of history, with the associated conserving activities: the museum, recollection through research, the preservation of monuments. Thus it is precisely the society that wears smock frocks that at the same time cares for plants and for traditional costumes. No age has destroyed as much as the modern period has, and no age has preserved as much as the modern period has, by developing skills that enable it to bring more and more of where it comes from with it into what is to come. That is why the modern age, in particular, has seen the origin of the appreciation of history and, beginning with Rousseau, of the appreciation of ecology, which are both assisted, in their compensatory tasks, by the human sciences' telling of preserving stories.

Orienting Stories. Here the issue—in terms of compensation for the world's increasing unfathomableness and coldness—is the need for a life-world that has meaning. Modernization has a disorienting effect, and this is compensated, again in modern times, by the encouragement of traditions with which one can identify: for example, the tradition of Christianity, the tradition of Humanism, the tradition of the Enlightenment, and so on. That is why the modern age, in particular, has seen the origin of a philosophical appreciation of historical orientations, including an appreciation of the relevance of historical orientations to ethics—and these are appreciations that are assisted, in their compensatory tasks, by the human sciences' telling of orienting stories. Here, however, it is not only a matter of identifying with traditions, but equally a matter of gaining distance from traditions, a subject on which I will now make some separate remarks in the following section.

In Praise of Ambiguity

The more modern the modern world becomes, the more unavoidable the human sciences become: and specifically as storytelling sciences. But are sciences allowed to tell stories?

The theory of science, whose representative spokespersons tend (today, just as they did at the end of the nineteenth century) to criticize the human sciences for being different from the experimental sciences—this theory of science is overwhelmingly opposed to storytelling. It recommends a piece of cosmetic surgery by which storytelling (and thereby the human sciences themselves) would be amputated from the human sciences. But that, in my opinion, does not speak against the storytelling science. Quite the reverse: It speaks against the theory of science. At the moment one of my jobs is to represent the philosophical profession in deliberations concerning its function and financing, and in this role I am of course prepared to defend the theory of science to my last drop of blood. As a philosopher, on the other hand, I am prepared to defend the theory of science—which seldom takes notice of the reality of science, and is (not least for that reason) an anemic affair—only to its own last drop of blood. In my view, a definition of the sciences that is more convincing, even today, than the (surrogate) definition provided by the theory of science, is their cooptative self-definition through scientific usual practices, according to which science is what recognized scientists recognize as science. The philosophy of the sciences provides orienting assistance for such acts of recognition precisely when it tells the story of how and in what historical contexts the sciences become what they are; as (for example) I am doing here, in the form of an ultrashort story, for the human sciences, with the thesis (so far) that the modernization that is driven by the experimental sciences causes losses on the level of the life-world, losses for which the human sciences help to compensate, so that they become more and more unavoidable, the more modern the modern world becomes. When, in this way, the science of science itself tells stories (and this is what the philosophy of science is presently tending toward doing), then the question as to whether sciences are allowed to tell stories has been settled in favor of the affirmative; from which it follows that what the human sciences need most of all is not the cosmetic surgery advised by a certain theory of science, but more courage to be themselves.

This also holds true in connection with the problem of univocity of meaning. We are told that people who tell stories fall short of the univocity of meaning at which sciences aim, so that the human sciences fall into ambiguity. But someone who makes this an objection against the human sciences overlooks something important, which is the fact that in the interpretive human sciences, and disregarding such (admittedly very important) auxiliary operations as the criticism of sources, dating, and the like, univocity is not an ideal that is not attained but a danger that has to be escaped. One has to notice what it was that ambiguity or multiple meaning was needed to oppose, and that it cost enormous exertion and—literally—blood, sweat, and tears precisely to get free of univocity.[8] For the human sciences are also—and precisely in their turning to ambiguity or multiple meaning—a late answer to the murderous experience of the religious civil wars, which were hermeneutic civil wars, because in them people killed one another in disputes about the unambiguously correct interpretation of a book, namely, the Holy Scriptures, the Bible. And this answer was a late one because it was only made inescapable by the murderous experience of the neoreligious civil wars that the modern revolutions since 1789 are—revolutions that remain hermeneutic civil wars because in them people killed and kill one another in disputes about the unambiguously correct interpretation of the one sole univocal world history. When two human groups assert, in controversy, that this book, the absolute book, which is all-important, and this history, the absolute history, which is all-important, admit only one unique and solely correct interpretation, and that we and only we have this interpretation, then the result can be hermeneutic homicide. The turning to ambiguity or multiple meaning responds precisely to this situation by asking: Could not this book and this history be interpreted differently, as well, and if that is not enough, in another different way and again and again in different ways?[9] This turning softens potentially deadly interpretive controversies by turning dogmatically univocal ways of understanding into interpreting and reinterpreting ways, and it discovers that books do not have only one interpretation and there is not only one book, and that histories do not have only one interpretation and there is not only one history. The human sciences "are" this discovery. They answer the trauma of the hermeneutic civil war—which originates in the dogmatism, grown furious, of univocity—by developing the salutary achievement that is ambiguity or multiple meaning. That is why they have to tell and retell stories. The result is the genesis of and the boom in philology (which is the discovery of the diversity of languages and books), and the genesis of and the boom in historicism (which is the discovery of the diversity of stories and their hermeneutic multiplicity of meaning). Thus, the turning from emphatic univocity to the human sciences' cultivation of ambiguity or multiple meanings becomes necessary as a response to the trauma of the hermeneutic civil war; so that ambiguity is not a misdeed in science but a good deed in the life-world (and in the "death-world").

This, too, is evidence for my fundamental thesis: This cultivation of diversity and of multiple meanings becomes unavoidable (and more and more so) precisely in modern times. For, as I suggested earlier, modernizations are dehistoricizations, so that they in particular—and thus modern times, in particular—create the danger that, when all stories are ruled out, in this way, one sole story may be left, the "progress" story of the ruling out of all other stories, which then becomes the exclusive story. Then human beings (each of them separately, and all of them together) are only allowed to have this one, unique story. But that, in my opinion, is antihuman. For these human beings need many stories (and many books and many interpretations) in order to be individuals: protected from the exclusive grip of a unique story, and thus free to be different, thanks to stories that are different in each case. It is just the human sciences (themselves also modern phenomena) that maintain this against the modern danger of the tendency toward an exclusive story. Here, in my (skeptic's) opinion, skepticism is at work in the human sciences; for skepticism is an appreciation of the separation of powers: all the way from doubt (understood as the separation of powers that is constituted by convictions), by way of the political separation of powers, to the separation of powers that is constituted by stories, books, and interpretations. Thus it is precisely in modern times that this separation of powers—the appreciation of historical variety and multiplicity of meaning, and of the liberating effect of the general motleyness of the reality of life—becomes increasingly necessary, against the danger of the exclusive and now only univocal story (or "history"); so that the rule holds, for this reason also, that the more modern the modern world becomes, the more unavoidable the human sciences become. They help us to emigrate from a world that is only objectified or whose story is only the story of progress; and because they do this, the human sciences have to do with education— because education ensures one's capacity to emigrate.

A New Opportunity for Anthropology?

All the human sciences [*Geisteswissenschaften*] are sciences of man [*Wissenschaften vom Menschen*]. But not all the sciences of man are human sciences. For there are also natural sciences (some of them experimental sciences) of man—the great example being the central disciplines of human medicine; and one of the important sciences of man is biology. It might be useful to concern ourselves with the question of how the sciences that deal with man—including the pragmatic action-guiding sciences: jurisprudence, economics, psychology, pedagogy, sociology, possibly theology, too—could be released from their isolations in pragmatic, natural-science and human-science contexts and brought together to collaborate. This intention has led again and again to the idea of a total science of the "whole human being"; and the traditional modern name for this total science of the "whole human being" is "anthropology."

In this connection, Wolf Lepenies has pointed out an important fact, namely, that the institutionalization of this total science of human beings, "anthropology"—of which the historians of disciplines know that the heyday of its dreams of glory was the first half of the nineteenth century—failed, in the second half of the nineteenth century.[10] Paradoxically, the slow victory of evolutionary over classificatory thinking, in that period, had the consequence that anthropology became both possible, in a way that it had never been before, and apparently superfluous. Darwin, for example, decreed that "man is no exception" in comparison to other living creatures; and thus the successful institutionalization, in the nineteenth century, was of biology rather than of anthropology. The theme of man's special features and peculiarities was excluded from biology, and the human sciences took it up. Thus—and here we could have in mind the following sequence of publication dates: 1859, Darwin's *Origin of Species;* 1871, Darwin's *Descent of Man;* 1883, Dilthey's *Einleitung in die Geisteswissenschaften* [Introduction to the Human Sciences]—the final theoretical and institutional success of the human sciences, toward the end of the nineteenth century, was in a way a consequence of the failed institutionalization of anthropology.

This development—the noninstitutionalization of anthropology as a comprehensive field—is not a misfortune. Not only were the human sciences able to continue to develop, freely and in motley variety, the social sciences were also able to complete their puberty in at least a partial disciplinary quarantine. At the same time evolutionary biology was also able to learn, independently, that the success of the idea of development (in which, while possible developments can indeed be found by throwing dice, actual developments have to be narrated) turns it, too—like the evolutionary Big Band cosmology—into a story-telling science. For the present, this tendency toward what one might call the "assimilation of the natural sciences to the human sciences" remains imperfect only because evolution, so far, is told only as the exclusive story that culminates in man. This "anthropic principle" constitutes the same difficulty for the theory of evolution that Eurocentrism constituted for the theory of progress in the philosophy of history. Perhaps the Ranke of evolutionary biology is already at work, somewhere, with the thesis that "every species has an immediate relation to God"; in any case, the theory of evolution still has its historicism—or, in other words, a still stronger tendency toward the "assimilation of the natural sciences to the human sciences"—ahead of it.[b] It is just this that I think offers an important new opportunity to bring together the sciences that deal with man—which is a process in which the human sciences would be in a strong position. For here again the rule is that the more modern the modern world becomes, the more unavoidable the human sciences become.

To be sure, it seems to me that the appropriate way, at the end of our century, to cultivate this motivation toward anthropology—toward a total science of man—is precisely not to institutionalize it as a field, but to actualize it through conversation that crosses the boundaries of fields: through interdisciplinary conversation.

This interdisciplinary conversation of the sciences that deal with man does not first have to be invented, and then laboriously put into action, for—at least in the form of a currently growing flood of pertinent interdisciplinary projects, colloquia, and workplaces—it has long since been present in reality; and experience shows that, as a rule, it is not impeded by communication difficulties caused by specialization, as long as these are not artificially induced by the perfectionism of communication, which is the true enemy of interdisciplinary conversation. For consensus is by no means always necessary; what is much more valuable is productive misunderstanding; and most valuable of all is simple reason: the abandonment of the effort to remain stupid. Even for me—a philosophical pro—it was at first surprising to find that philosophers are disproportionately well-represented in the interdisciplinary conversation between the special sciences that deal with man. Apparently philosophers bring with them from the tradition of their discipline—a two and a half thousand year old tradition of not arriving at agreement on fundamental positions—something that is useful in interdisciplinary discussion, namely, the ability to live with open aporias and surpluses of nonconsensus. The philosophers' ancient vice, as a profession—their chronic deficit of consensus—turns out to be an ultramodern interdisciplinary virtue: above all, a proficiency in surviving conversational confusion without discouragement. Philosophers are useful in other pertinent ways as well, for as far as competence for a specific zone of reality is concerned, they have no fixed hunting ground; instead, they have a universal poaching license. The philosopher is not an expert, but the expert's stuntman: his double in dangerous situations. His interdisciplinary usefulness as a conversational catalyst is connected to this ability to serve as a double for experts (who, after all, are harder to replace than philosophers) in situations that reach the level of risk, which is in fact characteristic of interdisciplinary conversations among the sciences that deal with man.

In my opinion, the major unsolved problem, so far, in connection with this current boom in interdisciplinary conversations among the sciences that deal with man is how it can be brought back into the universities. For there, within the universities, is where these conversations, at least predominantly, no longer occur. That may be due to the fact that, at least in this country, the resources for promoting interdisciplinary undertakings are mostly located and have their effect outside the universities, and also to changes in university structures that have driven these interdisciplinary conversations out of the universities. It is not an accident that it was exactly when the last interdisciplinary agencies, the "faculties," disappeared from the universities that the present boom in scientific tourism began, more or less as a substitute for them. Since then, interprofessional conversations in the sciences that deal with man have become the business of another place, as far as the universities are concerned. So one continues to be at the university, but one's thinking now takes place somewhere else. The question—which I will only pose here, and will not answer—is whether things should remain that way (and whether, for example, the demographic impact of the Pill, when it reaches the university, would not be an opportunity to change things). For the time being this is the situation: Because the university itself offers too few opportunities in this regard (not even relieving people of duties so as to offset additional interdisciplinary work), the researchers—and this certainly does not hold for the human scientists alone—disappear more and more frequently into the interworlds of transregional and, on occasion, intercontinental interdisciplinary work. I suspect that in the meantime this interdisciplinary tendency to go elsewhere has reached not only university teachers but chancellors and presidentss as well. When all that they do where duty obliges them to reside is to administer, they can only think when they are traveling, so they have to travel a great deal: for example, right now, to Bamberg, if only in order (among other things) to listen, with a patience for which I am grateful, to the thesis that I have advocated here (and supplemented in conclusion with a glance at the interdisciplinary work of the sciences that deal with man); that thesis being that the more modern the modern world becomes, the more unavoidable the human sciences become.[c]

Author's Notes

1. "Die Aufgabe der Geisteswissenschaften in der modernen Gesellschaft," in J. Ritter, *Subjektivität. Sechs Aufsätze* (Frankfurt, 1974), pp. 105–40.
2. Cf. A. Heuss, "Vom richtigen und falschen Bewusstsein. Geisteswissenschaft und Öffentlichkeit," in *Frankfurter Allgemeine Zeitung,* no. 34 (Febuary 9, 1985).
3. I borrow the phrase, "crisis of excessive demand" from H. Lübbe's introduction to H. Lübbe, ed., *Wozu Philosophie? Stellungnahmen eines Arbeitskreises* (Berlin and New York, 1978), p. VII, where he uses it to characterize the present situation of philosophy.
4. Cf. O. Marquard, "Kompensation. Überlegungen zu einer Verlaufsfigur geschichtlicher Prozesse," in K. G. Faber and Ch. Meier, eds., *Historische Pro-*

zesse, Theorie der Geschichte, vol. 2 (Munich, 1978), pp. 330–62; and O. Marquard, "Glück im Unglück. Zur Theorie des indirekten Glücks zwischen Theodizee und Geschichtsphilosophie," in G. Bien, ed., Die Frage nach dem Glück (Stuttgart, 1978), pp. 93–111. See also, since then, J. Svagelski, L'Idée de compensation en France, 1750–1850 (Lyon, 1981), as well as O. Marquard, "Homo compensator," in G. Frey and J. Zelger, eds., Der Mensch und die Wissenschaften vom Menschen, vol. 1 (Innsbruck, 1983), pp. 55–66.

5. Cf. H. Blumenberg, Die Lesbarkeit der Welt (Frankfurt, 1981).

6. Cf. especially H. Lübbe, Geschichtsbegriff und Geschichtsinteresse. Analytik und Pragmatik der Historie (Basel and Stuttgart, 1977), p. 22: "In view of these connections, Joachim Ritter ascribed to the historiographical human sciences the cultural function of compensating for the 'real historilessness' of the modern world. This suggestion is accepted in the last chapter of the present book, but with the not unimportant nuance that here the 'real historilessness' is interpreted, less misleadingly, as the historically unparalleled historicalness—i.e., the structure-altering dynamism—of our civilization." See also pp. 304ff., and also R. Koselleck, Vergangene Zukunft. Zur Semantik geschichtlicher Zeiten (Frankfurt, 1979), translated by K. Tribe as Futures Past: On the Semantics of Historical Time (Cambridge, Mass., 1985).

7. "What man is, is something that only his history tells him": W. Dilthey, "Traum," in Gesammelte Werke (Leipzig and Berlin, 1913–), vol. 8, ed. B. Groethuysen (1931), p. 224. "The story stands for the man": W. Schapp, In Geschichten verstrickt (1953); 2nd ed. Wiesbaden, 1976), p. 108.

8. Cf. O. Marquard, "The Question: To What Question is Hermeneutics the Answer," in Farewell to Matters of Principle, translated by Robert M. Wallace (Oxford, 1988), originally published as Abschied vom Prinzipiellen (Stuttgart, 1981). Also, O. Marquard, Krise der Erwartung—Stunde der Erfahrung. Zur ästhetischen Kompensation des modernen Erfahrungsverlustes (Konstanz, 1982).

9. Cf. the "reception history" approach, of which H. R. Jauss, Ästhetische Erfahrung und literarische Hermeneutik (Frankfurt, 1982) [part one translated by M. Shaw as Aesthetic Experience and Literary Hermeneutics (Minneapolis, 1982)], is representative.

10. Cf. W. Lepenies, Das Ende der Naturgeschichte. Wandel kultureller Selbstverständlichkeit in den Wissenschaften des 18. und 19. Jahrhunderts (Frankfurt, 1978); and W. Lepenies, "Naturgeschichte und Anthropologie im 18. Jahrhundert," in B. Fabian, W. Schmidt-Biggemann, and R. Vierhaus, eds., Deutschlands kulturelle Entfaltung. Die Neubestimmung des Menschen, Studien zum achtzehnten Jahrhundert, vols. 2 and 3 (Munich, 1980), pp. 211–26.

11. Cf. O. Marquard, "Zur Geschichte des philosophischen Begriffs 'Anthropologie' seit dem Ende des 18. Jahrhunderts," in O. Marquard, Schwierigkeiten mit der Geschichtsphilosophie (1973; 2nd ed. Frankfurt, 1982), pp. 122–44.

Translator's Notes

a. "Challenge" and "response" (Arnold Toynbee's terms) are in English in the original.

b. For Ranke's original dictum, see the second section of chapter 2, "Unburdenings," and the author's note 9. (And on the non-Popperian sense in which Marquard uses the term "historicism," see translator's note b to "Skeptics" in chapter 1.)

c. This paper was the opening address of the 1985 annual conference of the West German Conference of University Presidents (Westdeutsche Rektorenkonferenz), May 5, 1985, in Bamberg.

=7=

In Defense of the Accidental: Philosophical Reflections on Man

Accident seems to be one of the worst enemies of man's freedom and dignity. Nevertheless, I would like to put in a good word here for accident, and for its results. Am I then speaking against man's freedom and dignity? By no means. It is just that I think that it would be a sign of deficiency of freedom if man were to live undignifiedly beyond his means: beyond the means, that is, of his finite nature. If he chooses not to do this, he has to acknowledge the results of accident, by a defense of the accidental. This is my thesis here.[1]

Almost the entire philosophical tradition seems to contradict this thesis. I quote: "Philosophical reflection has no other object than to get rid of what is accidental." This is Hegel's summing up of the traditional opinion.[2] It is seldom, and reluctantly, that I contradict that great empiricist, Hegel. But here I am doing it, by necessity. To get rid of what is accidental would mean, for example, to get rid of philosophers; but without philosophers (whether they are amateur or professional makes no difference) there would be no philosophy, so that in the end one would rid philosophy, in the name of philosophy, of philosophy. So the accidental has to be retrieved for philosophy; for it is only through it that philosophy has reality. To get rid of what is accidental would also mean, for example, to rid man of all his-too-humanness; but without all-too-humanness, there is no man; so that one would finally rid man, in the name of man, of man. So the accidental has to be retrieved for man; for it is only through it that man has reality.

In what follows I cannot execute this plea for the accidental in a comprehensive manner; I can only contribute some relevant and (as is fitting in dealing with the accidental) accidental considerations, which I will do in four sections, under the following headings: the program of making man absolute, and its modern pronounced form; on the unavoidability of usual practices; we human beings are always more our accidents than our choices; and human freedom depends on the separation of powers.

The Program of Making Man Absolute, and Its Modern Pronounced Form

When—to begin with Hegel's formulation—"philosophical reflection has no other object than to get rid of what is accidental," then philosophy's program becomes (and the more modern the circumstances, the more pronouncedly is this the case) the program of making man absolute.

As a countermove against this program of making man absolute—which is an old program, which only became more pronounced in modern times—philosophical attempts were made to arrive at an understanding of accident and its results, beginning with Aristotle's acceptance (in contrast to the Megarian school's denial) of the accidental as what is neither impossible nor necessary, and thus could also be different or not.[3] This realm of the accidental (or the contingent)[4] became a problem in at least three ways: as an opponent of the necessary; as the foundation of the necessary; or in other ways as well. Here are three short remarks on these possibilities.

"*Si necessarium, unde contingens?*" [If there is something necessary, whence comes the contingent?] This question—whose pronounced form is: If God, after all, exists, why do finite things exist?—leads, in the Christian tradition in philosophy, to the problem of the contingency of the Creation,[5] and later (when, beginning with Spinoza, nature occupies the divine position of necessity), to the problem of freedom and the question of the undetermined. Perhaps accident is a necessity that miscarried.

"*Si contingens, unde necessarium?*" [If there is something contingent, whence comes the necessary?] This question, which picks up motives of Epicurus's doctrine of the declination of the atoms and Darwin's doctrine of mutation, has recently been radicalized (following, for example, Monod[6]) and thus given contemporary significance in the theory of evolution and synergy: If chaos exists, why is there order, and if accidental things exist, where do necessary ones come from? Perhaps necessity is successful accident.

To illustrate the third possibility, let us note that Aristotle was also the first to see that accidents can come about through the unexpected mutual encounter of chains of determining events that are independent of one another. One person buries a treasure in order to hide it; another person digs a hole in order to plant a tree: "It is an accident for a person who is digging a hole to find a treasure in doing so." A special case, and an important one for human beings, is when something else (which in its turn is determined) interferes with purposes that they have: "Going to Aegina was an accident for a man, if he went not in order to get there, but because he was carried out of his way by a storm or captured by pirates."[7] Something happens to us that we did not intend or choose. For we human beings are not only our (intention-guided) actions, but also our accidents.

The program of making man absolute denies this: It wants above all to "get rid of" the accidents of the last kind also, so that (and here I use Sartre's formula of the "choice, that we are"[8]) it will be the case that human beings are, without exception, not their accidents, but only and completely their choice. This means two things. First, man is, or should be, exclusively the outcome of his intentions. He is then the acting creature, to whom nothing happens any longer. Nothing human is allowed to be unintended; nothing human is allowed to happen without having been chosen. Nothing is allowed to befall man any longer. For only then is it the case that human beings are not their accidents but only and completely their choice. Second, this choice has to be absolute: that is, not an accidental option that could also have been different, that could be replaced by other intentions. Consequently all human beings—if they want to be proper (that is, absolute) human beings—must cherish the same intentions. For only then is it the case that human beings are not their accidents, but only and completely their absolute choice.

I am sometimes asked, Who exactly is it, then, in philosophy, who advocated or advocates this program of making man absolute? Marquard, name the horse and the rider! Now, it may be that the person who asks this is himself among the horses, and the tradition that rides him is what I am describing right now (if only in ultrabrief form). Moreover, there are good reasons to take pains to neglect these details: A short lecture cannot get involved with questions of philology—of Plato's philology, Augustine's philology, Descartes's philology, Fichte's philology, Marx's, Apel's, and Habermas's philology. Also, tactfulness enjoins us to allow philosophers (the more so, the more modern they are) the conviction that they are not the ones intended. In any case, we are not among poor people here; if need be, I will invent German Idealism (including Marxism and Neo-Marxism) myself. That is also the reason why I forbid no one the impression that the position that I have sketched here and which I attack in what follows—the program of making man absolute—has never been advocated by anyone. For would that be bad? Quite the contrary: It would be, precisely, good for my defense of the accidental if it had fewer opponents than I had assumed. In short: The question to whom to attribute the program of making man absolute leaves plenty of room for discussion.

However, one can certainly say what I already said: that the program of making man absolute, a program that is old in (and not only in) philosophy, is intensified, takes a more pronounced form, in modern times. When, in modern times, one no longer likes to rely on a participation in God which guarantees man's absoluteness (his accident-free and absolutely correct life), the process of making man absolute must increasingly be founded on man himself: on his freedom, his own absolute choice. The fact that it was above all German philosophy (in German Idealism and in Marxism) that played the leading role here can be understood with the help of Plessner's theses about the "delayed nation"[9]: The retardation of liberal arrangements in the realm of reality is compensated for by absoluteness in the realm of philosophy. Thus it is precisely in modern times that (also because God, as a moderating quantity, increasingly drops out of philosophy) we arrive—following the program of making man absolute, and continuing with the Sartrean formula that I quoted—at the definition of man as the absolute choice that he is. Thus human beings are supposed to be, or to become, absolute.

However, human beings are not absolute; rather, they are finite. They live and they do not (at least not preponderantly) choose their life absolutely, and this is because they have to die. To use Heidegger's words, they are "toward death."[10] A limit is fixed to their lives: "vita brevis." Human life is too short for an absolute choice. On the most elementary level, human beings simply do not have enough time absolutely to choose, or to choose to reject, what they (accidentally) already are, and to choose (or even absolutely to choose), instead of that, something entirely different and new. Their death is always swifter than their absolute choice. Thus the program of making man absolute is opposed by man's reality, which bears the stamp of mortality; and in what follows I would like—through a defense of the accidental—to promote a recognition of this fact by philosophy.

On the Unavoidability of Usual Practices

I repeat: The program of making man absolute is opposed by man's reality, which bears the stamp of mortality. Consequently part of the program of making man absolute is an attempt to abrogate the human reality that opposes it: in the Greek tradition, to declare that reality not genuine; or, in the Christian tradition, to declare that reality temporary, already judged, and subject to eschatological recall; or—in the program's modern, pronounced form—to bracket that reality out, precautionally and methodically.

The representative modern attempt at bracketing the reality out in that way—at suspending human reality, as long as it is not the absolute reality—is so-called methodical doubt. Descartes developed this attempt, for the realm of theory, in his *Meditationes.*[11] Descartes's rule of doubt lays down: *in dubio contra traditionem* [in case of doubt, reject tradition]. In other words: Everything that is not absolutely true, and

could therefore be false (which is all of our present judgmental knowledge), is to be treated as though it were really false, and it is to be treated
this way until it has been shown—through *scientia more certa methodo*
[the sure method of science]—"clare et distincte," that is, absolutely, to
be true. As long as this has not been done, all judgment has to be
suspended. For all judgments are not, for example, permitted until they
are forbidden as a result of their falsification; instead, they are prohibited until they are permitted as a result of their absolute verification.
Knowledge remains suspended as long as it is not absolute knowledge.
The theorists of discourse ethics—that is, for example, Apel and
Habermas—have carried this methodical doubt over to the practical
realm: Discourse ethics applies methodical doubt to norms of action, as
well.[12] Its rule of suspicion lays down: *in dubio contra traditionem (sive
conventiones)* [in case of doubt, reject tradition (or conventions)]. In
other words: Everything that is not demonstrably (by the consensus of a
dominance-free discourse)—that is, absolutely—good, and which
could therefore be evil (which is to say, all of our present orientations for
action), is to be treated as though it were really evil, and it is to be treated
this way until it has been justified, through the absolute discourse,
consensually—that is, absolutely—as good. As long as this has not been
done, all convention-guided action must be suspended and, to help
make this possible, suspected. It is not that practical orientations in life
are permitted until they are forbidden as a result of their demonstrated
badness; instead, they are prohibited until they are absolutely permitted
as a result of their discursive legitimation. Thus in both cases—in Descartes and in discourse ethics—what is present is negated as a precau-
tion: The "usual" (knowledge that is accepted because it was accepted
in the past, and instructions for action that are accepted because they
were accepted in the past) is methodically canceled out in the name of
the absolute. Overall, the rule—in this negative side of the program of
making man absolute—is that life should be discontinued (and, to help
make this possible, seen as bad) as long as it has not been shown absolutely, by absolute choice (absolute knowledge, absolute justification of
action), that it is the absolutely correct life. The program of making man
absolute negates real life, precautionally, insofar as real life is the ensemble of usual practices.

Of course, this negative side of the program of making man absolute cannot succeed either. It, too, is frustrated by human finitude, by mortality. Human beings have to die, they are "toward death." Apart from any existentialist emphasis, this statement is philosophically central; and it can in fact be expressed quite unemphatically, as follows: In the total human population, the rate of mortality comes to 100 percent. But death, however long it may hesitate, always comes all too soon: Human life is too short for executing the program of making man absolute, because death does not allow us time to wait for the result of the absolute choice of all the orientations that are necessary for life. But if, at the same time, the orientations for life that are present, as a matter of historical fact, and that are not absolutely chosen but are only usual practices, are abrogated until absolute choice has finished absolutely choosing all the absolute orientations that are necessary for life—then this amounts, in effect, for human beings, to a prohibition of beginning life before it is over; because, as I said, our death is always swifter than our absolute choice.

Thus one can say that for human beings, the program of making man absolute is a philosophy for their life after death, and it leaves open the question of a philosophy for their life before death. But it is precisely for their life before death that human beings need philosophy. If, then, the absolute philosophy does not yet exist (because of the absolute time required by its absolute choice), and if our usual practices no longer exist (because of their absolute methodical negation: their subjection to doubt and suspicion), then evidently a temporary substitute orientation in life is needed, which will step into this temporal gap that is our life. For Descartes, in the third part of his *Discours,* precisely that became the argument for the so-called "provisional ethic."[13] His image was that if one tears down a house in order to build a new one, one has to arrange for temporary lodgings. In my opinion, this is true not only (as Descartes thought) in regard to ethics, but also in regard to knowledge and to human orientations in life, in general. Consequently, in the case (also) of the general program of making man absolute, and especially in that case, the generalized counterpart of the provisional ethic—namely, a philosophy of provisional orientations in life—must become a matter of present interest.

Of course, as soon as this philosophy (the philosophy of human life not after, but before death) makes its appearance in the name of the program of making man absolute—as, so to speak, a measure taken to protect the flank of absolute choice—it winds up in an aporia. For either the provisional orientations in life are not themselves products of absolute choice, in which case they also are subject to the latter's methodical negation of usual practices, or else the provisional orientations in life are, after all, themselves products of absolute choice, in which case they, in their turn, will require us (more or less absolutely) to wait for them, and will once again need, as a temporary substitute orientation, further provisional orientations in life, and so on. A weaker form of this aporia also arises even if the temporary orientation is supposed to be a comprehensive new invention of a different kind, containing only a provisional minimum of all the orientations that are necessary in life: Then, too, it reproduces the problem that it was meant to solve. The only situation in which this is not the case, and in which the aporia that I have described disappears, is if the provisional orientations in life are identical with the orientations in life that are present in fact—that is, with the existing usual practices[14]— and if one does not methodically negate these existing usual practices. From which I conclude that the philosophy of provisional orientations in life, which we are seeking, is none other than the philosophy of the existing usual practices—which is a philosophy that asserts that we cannot live without these existing usual practices (traditions, mores, usages in knowledge and in action); that with or without a program of making man absolute, these practices cannot be bypassed: they are unavoidable. The choice that we are is supported by them as the nonchoice that we are: What is to come requires what we come from; choice requires usual practices. In no way does this mean that all traditions must always remain untouched and all usual practices un- altered, since, on the contrary, usual practices are quite capable of being changed and reformed. All that it means is that more usual practices must always be upheld than are changed, otherwise our life is ruined; and that the burden of proof (which can certainly be borne, successfully, again and again) is always on the advocate of change.[15] It is in this sense (and only in this sense) that usual practices are unavoidable for human beings: We human beings are always more our usual practices than our choice, and still more are we always more our usual practices than our *absolute* choice. Accordingly, a nonabsolute, human philosophy has to be just this: a defense of usual practices.

That is why one also has to defend usual practices—the things that are accepted because (as the "usual") they were accepted in the past—against slanderous talk, even if this talk puts on philosophically absolute airs. It is not the case that the reality of the modern world—because its accelerating rate of change increases the tempo of obsolescence—continually puts all usual practices in question and wears them away; for precisely in the modern world there are compensating stabilities, not least of all in the fact that in it, just because of its increasing speed of obsolescence, the obsolescences themselves also become more and more rapidly obsolete. Besides, modernization itself has long since become a usual practice: the usage of modernity. At the same time, I find increasingly dubious the argument against usual practices that one can call the "Eichmann argument," and which says that someone whose life is guided by usual practices is in direct danger of becoming an Eichmann—Eichmann being a person who after all only wanted to do his usual duty.[16] It seems to me that here only the second aspect of Eichmann's monstrous actions is taken into account, and that the first aspect consisted in his violation of a usual practice: the usual practice of not murdering one's fellow human beings. I cannot go into detail here on the Eichmann case and the debate about the "banality of evil,"[17] but in my view this primary deviation from the usual was secondarily camouflaged, by the perpetrator (camouflaged, in the end, from himself as well), by the consciousness that he was more than fulfilling his usual duty. This does not, in my opinion, count as an argument against usual practices, any more than it counts as an argument against the kind of truthfulness that says that lying, in order to be successful, must pretend to be, and camouflage itself as, truthfulness (and that the pretense and camouflage can extend, if need be, even to the liar). *Abusus non tollit usum:* Misuse does not refute use. Eichmann's bureaucratically perpetrated crimes suffered not from an excess but from a deficiency of usual practices: The "Eichmann" danger is, in my opinion, greater when one begins by putting all usual practices up for grabs (even if it is in the name of the absolute or of some other good cause), than when one refuses to do this. It is useful to remember that opposition came above all from groups with intact traditions.[a] That is why it is also not correct to say that setting store by usual practices makes critique impossible; because the opposite is the case. Critique is, above all, conflict between usual practices. To be capable of it, one must *have* usual practices; and in our times and our parts of the world critique is in fact itself a usual practice, which is regulated by usual practices.

We must (I repeat) defend usual practices against slander, and consequently we must also defend them against the jaundiced view of usual practices that is produced by the perfectionistic deontological demands of the program of making man absolute. In his critique of deontological thinking, Hegel showed that deontological hypertrophy has the effect of spoiling what exists.[18] Likewise, someone who grants validity only to the absolute's absolute choice treats the existing usual practices unfairly. But usual practices should not be demonized: The fact that they are not heaven on earth, the absolutely good, is not enough to make them hell on earth, the absolutely bad (as though there were nothing in between that it is worthwhile to be concerned about and to defend). Precisely because today's world is—undeniably—difficult, we need a sharpened appreciation of the difference between what is simply bad, and the existing reality: We need, that is, a philosophical defense of usual practices.

We Human Beings Are Always More Our Accidents Than Our Choice

The program of making man absolute warns that, measured against the absolute, usual practices are accidental. As I see it, while that is true, it is not an objection. It becomes an objection as a result of a misconception, according to which what is accidental is always optional, something that can be arbitrarily chosen or rejected. It is certainly true that arbitrary optionalness is not a characteristic that can reasonably be imputed to orientations in life—in action, knowledge, and living. If one can continually exchange one orientation for another, the things being exchanged are not orientations; and if the accidental were only the arbitrarily optional, this would indeed have ruinous consequences, both for usual practices, which are indeed accidental, and for human life, for which usual practices are unavoidable. However, it is just not the case that the accidental is solely the arbitrarily optional.

The concept of the accidental—that is, the contingent—as finite, which derives from the Christian theology of creation and is summarized in the formulas "contingens est, quod nec est impossibile nec necessarium" [the contingent is what is neither impossible nor necessary], or "contingens est, quod potest non esse" [the contingent is what could not-be],[19] does indeed mean that which could also not be, or which could also be different; but if one sees this not from the perspective of God, the Creator, but, more humanly, from the perspective of the life-world and man, it comes in two different forms.[20] *Either,* that is, the accidental is "that which could also be different" and which *we can change* (for example, one can drink tea, or refrain from drinking tea and instead eat bologna; and this lecture might also not be your cup of tea, because it is bologna, or it could also not be given at all, or be given in a different way). This kind of accidental thing, as "what could also be different" and which we could change, is an arbitrarily choosable or rejectable object of discretion, which I would like to call the "arbitrarily accidental," or the arbitrary. *Or,* on the other hand, the accidental is "that which could also be different" and is *precisely not changeable by us* (blows of fate, by which I mean illnesses, being born, and the like). This kind of accidental thing, as "what could also be different" and is precisely not (or only slightly) changeable by us, is fate. It is resistant, to a high degree, to negation, and is not (or is scarcely) escapable. I would like to call it the "fatefully accidental," or the fateful. It follows, then, from this distinction, that there exist, for human beings, not only one type of accidentalness, but two: We have not only the arbitrarily accidental but also the fatefully accidental.

Now it seems to me that it is overwhelmingly accidents of this second kind (accidents, that is, of the "fatefully accidental" type), the natural and historical facts and events that befall us, that make up our life. This starts, to begin at the beginning, at our birth: We could also not have been born, or we could have been born at a different time, in a different part of the world, a different culture, a different situation in life; but once we are born, we can no longer annul all of that. Even a suicide happens *ex suppositione nativiatatis* [from the supposition of birth]. The fact that birth is a fateful accident is illuminated by Alfred Polgar's commentary on Silenus: "The best thing is not to be born—but who does that ever happen to?" Fateful accidents are the reality of our life, because as human beings we are always "entangled in stories" (Wilhelm Schapp); because, as Hermann Lübbe, above all, has shown, actions become stories when something interferes in them, happens to them, befalls them.[21] A story is a choice that is interrupted by something accidental, something fatefully accidental; this is why stories cannot be planned, but must be told. Our life is composed of these mixtures—which stories are—of our action and what befalls us; which is why the fatefully accidental element is predominant in it. It is also accidental, fatefully accidental, that we are subject to the natural laws that the natural sciences discover: We could also have been subject to other forms of determination, but we are in fact, accidentally, subject to these.[22] But just this is an accident that we cannot change: a fateful accident for man. The accident that affects us most fatefully and most severely—unless one regards it as the consolation of not having to go on performing our tricks forever—is our death. A fateful accident condemns us, by our birth, to death—that is, to the brevity of life that does not allow us the time to escape, as far as we might like, from what we accidentally already are. Our mortality forces us to "be"—that is, to remain, predominantly—the fateful accident that our past is for us. Part of this past is, decisively and essentially, the accidents that our usual practices are—practices that we do not choose, to begin with, but in which we are involved. They could be completely different, but, vita brevis, we cannot for the most part change them. It is not, after all, as though we first had to, as it were, seek them out; rather, we always already have them, and cannot (and do not need), for the most part, to get free of them. They are fateful accidents, and someone who accuses them (as in the absolute argumentation that is the norm in philosophy) of being arbitrarily optional, thinks and speaks right past them, and his argument is, to that extent, worthless. It is indeed true that the usual is accidental, but since it is not arbitrarily optional, this is not an objection to it. For our usual practices are certainly always more our accidents than our choice, but they are not arbitrarily accidental, but fatefully accidental.

I will only mention in passing the question of how human beings can live and deal with the accidental. One of the ways of dealing with arbitrarily accidental is certainly art: the use of form to reduce arbitrariness. And one of the ways of dealing with the fatefully accidental is certainly religion: the transformation of extreme situations into routines. Both of these, art and religion, attempt to master something; art (perhaps) masters arbitrary contingency, and religion (perhaps) masters fateful contingency.

In philosophy, then, it seems to me, people have focused on the arbitrarily accidental and forgotten the fatefully accidental, so as to deal quickly with the accidental and "get rid of" it easily. This is a natural thing to do if one cultivates only the absolute, or external, point of view in connection with accident, rather than insisting, phenomenologically, on the internal point of view—the view from the life-world—on the accidental, as well. For example, in the discussions of the accidental in the theology of creation, in stochastics, or in game theory, one seldom encounters the perspective of the person to whom the results of the creation or of other accidents are served up. There is also a modification of one's perspective on the accidental that is connected with one's position in terms of age. In the modern world—the age of tachogenic unworldliness, in which people increasingly do not grow up—the dominant perspective on the accidental is that of youth. Fear of arbitrariness is an optical illusion of youth, which only persists because of the rule that "there's no such thing as a grown-up person."[23] The experience of the preponderance and vital significance of the accidents that leave their imprint on us, although they are precisely not under our discretion (so that they are not arbitrary accidents, but fateful accidents), is an experience that is associated with age but which one can have early on in life, because it is also a rule that every human being, even the youngest, is already old—that is, is so close to death that he or she does not, in any case, have time to efface (to any considerable extent) the accidental quality of the accidents of which his or her life is composed.

It is, above all, this experience (an experience associated with age), of the dominance of what is fatefully accidental that has to be asserted in opposition to the program of making man absolute. Not only do we never give our lives a predominantly absolute necessity, by our choice, so that to that extent they remain accidental in the sense of the arbitrarily accidental, but beyond that, we cannot, in general, essentially choose (not to speak of absolutely choosing) our life and its reality, so that it also (and above all) remains accidental in the sense of what is fatefully accidental. It is more through accidents than through our choice (that is, our plans) that we get through life and become ourselves. And that is not, as the philosophy of absolute choice and of making man absolute wants to make us believe, a misfortune—because accident is not a failure of absoluteness, but (under conditions of mortality) our historically normal state. We human beings are always more our accidents than our choice. Note that I do not say that we human beings are only our accidents; I only say that we are not only our choice, and that we human beings are always more our accidents than our choice. Still more are we human beings always more our accidents than our *absolute* choice, and we have to accept that; for we are not absolute, but finite. A philosophy that—skeptically—insists upon this ineradicability of the accidental is, to that extent, a defense of the accidental.

Human Freedom Depends upon the Separation of Powers

One could sum up our results, so far, in these propositions: Part of man's dignity is his ability to bear the accidental, and part of his freedom is his acknowledgment of the accidental. This implies, positively, that respect for human diginity is, above all, compassion, and that respect for human freedom is, above all, tolerance. At the same time it also implies, negatively, that man's dignity is not the dignity of an absolute diva, who is permanently offended by not being treated as God or—as one who is solely an end in himself—at least to some degree as God; and it implies that man's freedom is not (as the power of reason) absolute choice, for which there is nothing unchosen, nothing accidental. That human dignity nevertheless really is or can be dignity, and human freedom really is or can be freedom, is a result of the following, concluding reflections, which bring the separation of powers into play in this connection.

If what has been said so far is correct, man's reality is predominantly accidental. That which is accidental can also be different. But if it *can* be different, it frequently, if only accidentally, also *is* different: Accidental reality is—accidentally—often thus and also different; it embraces various things; it is multiform, motley. This very motleyness is the human opportunity for freedom. It is the possibility of freedom that is put in the foreground by the doctrine of the separation of powers; for the effect of the political separation of powers, in terms of political freedom, is only a special case of the effect of the general motleyness of reality, in terms of freedom in general—a special case of the effect of the fact that the accidents that befall man, as fates, are not uniform and monolithic, but instead—accidentally—intersect and interfere with one another and thus, to a degree, neutralize one another. It is true that in the famous section on the English Constitution in his *De l'Esprit des lois,*[24] Montesquieu put forward the separation of powers—as the division between the three political powers, the legislative, executive, and judicial—only as a guarantee of *political* freedom; but one should bear in mind that Montesquieu (who, incidentally, brought into play the motleyness of the conditions of human life in other areas as well, all the way to climate) belonged to the tradition of the moralists, and that they were part of the skeptical tradition.[25]

But skepticism is an appreciation of the separation of powers: Skepticism's doubt—as the word *Zweifel* [doubt] says (which, after all, contains the idea of multiplicity in its "zwei" [two])—is precisely the procedure, known in the skeptical tradition as "isosthenes diaphonia,"[26] of letting two opposed convictions collide with each other in such a way that both of them decline so much in power that the individual, as the laughing or crying third party, gets free of them. And what happens in this way with two convictions is still more the case with several convictions: Each of them distances the individual from the others. What is true of convictions is equally true of other forces, tendencies, magnitudes in reality: It is crucial, for the freedom that skepticism asserts (that is, for finite freedom), that there is never only one such power at work, but always a number of them, pluralistically competing, intersecting and interfering with one another, and thus reciprocally balancing one another. By codetermining man, each of them—so to speak—guarantees him latitude (distance) in relation to the others, and protects him from the sole determining clutches of a single power, in the face of which he would be powerless, on his own. The principle is: *"Divide et fuge!"* [Divide and escape!]. Thus it is advantageous for man, because of the consequences in terms of freedom, to have many (several) convictions: not no convictions at all, and not only one, but many. And it is advantageous for him to have many (several) traditions and stories, and also many souls (alas!) in his own breast: not no tradition, story, or soul at all, and not only one, but many. And perhaps it is also advantageous for him to have many (several) gods and points of orientation: not none at all, and not only one, but several or even many. In general, it is advantageous for man to have many determining factors: not none at all, and not only one, but many; because human beings are not free by virtue of the fact that they copy God (as quasi-omnipotent directors on the world stage, or by having unconditioned capability); rather, they are free through freedoms, in the plural, which fall to their lot because, in the crush of the determinants that bombard them, these determinants hinder each other, reciprocally, in their determining work. It is only by virtue of the fact that each further determinant curtails, impedes, and moderates the determining pressure of each of the others that each human being is and possesses his or her own (modest, entirely finite, limited) individual freedom vis-à-vis the sole clutches of each determinant. What makes a human being free is not zero determination—the absence of all determinants—or the superior force of a single determinant, but a superabundance of determinants.[27] So the thesis about the separation of powers (generalized in the spirit of skeptical moralism) that I put forward here is that overdetermination promotes freedom and, consequently, as I said already (and at the risk that all of this may become too motley for you), that the general motleyness of the natural and historical human reality promotes freedom. The circumstance that what befalls human beings, in the way of accident, is not one unique and indivisible accident, but instead accidents in the plural—this (itself fatefully accidental) circumstance brings it about that the human lot turns out, accidentally, to be freedom (in the form of freedoms, in the plural).

Thus what man has to fear is not determination, but the undividedness of its power. In this connection, his freedom (which consists in freedoms, in the plural) can rely on the aspect of reality that compensates, through motleyness, for compulsions to unity, and which thus also compensates not only for absolute universalizations and for modern uniformities and streamlinings, but for the harsh compulsion to uniqueness to which we are all subject because we have only one, unique life. For we can escape from that one life into communication with our fellow human beings (whom we need, for just that reason) through the possibility of sharing their lives (which are, of course, many) and thus pluralizing our own lives. Furthermore, it is in general important—so that their capacity for arresting determining powers can come into play, too—that the greatest possible number of determinants should be incorporated into our lives, which means incorporating, as well, the fatefully accidental pieces of reality that exercise their determining effect by being noticed. Thus it is advantageous for human beings when the boundaries of what they notice collapse. The most human (or even all-too-human) of these "extreme reactions" [Grenzreaktionen]—which are among those that, as "That's the way it is" reactions, constitute human reason, or the abandonment of the effort to remain stupid—are, as Helmuth Plessner and Joachim Ritter have shown, laughing and crying[28]: that is, the gentle ways in which we acknowledge previously unnoticed and repressed fateful accidents, which—balancing other determinants—codetermine human reality. By laughing or crying, we intimate our acceptance of what remained, officially, excluded from consideration, but is, unofficially, part of the story: namely, the accidents that (accidentally) thwart what is officially accepted. Through them, we laugh or cry ourselves free. Thus a readiness to laugh and a readiness to cry—that is, humor and melancholy—are concrete forms taken by tolerance and compassion. They are ways of honoring, both humanly and all-too-humanly, the freedom and dignity of man. One of the implications and results of my reflections is, then, that someone who can laugh and cry is free; and that someone who laughs and cries, and especially—among human beings—someone who has laughed and cried a lot, has dignity. So these extreme reactions, laughing and crying, are forms of what I wanted to draw attention to here: forms of the defense of the accidental.

Author's Notes

1. A short preliminary study on the same subject as what follows is O. Marquard, "Einwilligung in das Zufällige," *Neue Zürcher Zeitung*, no. 30, February 5–6, 1983, pp. 69–70. The chief thesis of that piece goes back to a text on "Differentiations in the Concept of Contingency," which I was unable to complete in 1976. The present piece also reflects some thinking that was developed more specifically in O. Marquard, "Das Über-Wir. Bemerkungen zur Diskursethik," in K. Stierle, R. Warning, eds., *Das Gespräch*, Poetik und Hermeneutik 11 (Munich, 1984), pp. 29–44.

2. G. W. F. Hegel, *Die Vernunft in der Geschichte* (1822, 1828, 1830), ed. G. Lasson (5th printing, Hamburg, 1955), p. 29.

3. See Aristotle, *Prior Analytics* I 13: 32 a 18–20.

4. I dealt with "Texts on the Problem of Contingency" in my seminar in the winter semester of 1985–1986 and in the summer semester of 1986, and I thank the active participants in this seminar for many suggestions. In what follows, I am concerned with only one part of the overall problematic. For the rest of it, I refer the reader to the work of my copilot in this seminar: F. J. Wetz's dissertation in progress, whose working title is "Faktizität—Ontologische Probleme von Zufall und Zeit" [Facticity—Ontological Problems of Accident and Time]. References to the literature may be found there.

5. Cf. H. Blumenberg, "Kontingenz," in *Die Religion in Geschichte und Gesellschaft*, vol. 3 (3rd ed., Tübingen, 1959), cols. 1793–94.

6. J. Monod, *Le hasard et la nécessité* (Paris, 1970); translated by A. Wainhouse as *Chance and Necessity* (New York, 1971).

7. Aristotle, *Metaphysics* IV 30: 1025 a 14–34, esp. 1617 and 25–27 (accidental = *symbebēkos*). Cf. Aristotle, *Physics* VI: 197 a 5–7. See also Boethius, *Philosophiae consolationis libri quinque* (524), esp. the beginning of the fifth book; in English, *The Consolations of Philosophy*, trans. W. J. Oates (New York, 1957), p. 50: "Such a thing is believed to have happened by chance, but not from nothing, for it has its own causes whose unforeseen and unexpected coincidence seems to have brought about a chance. . . . Chance therefore may

be defined as an unexpected result from the coincidence of certain causes in matters done for some other purpose."

8. J.-P. Sartre, *L'Être et le néant* (Paris, 1943), p. 638: "le choix que je suis."

9. Cf. H. Plessner, *Die verspätete Nation. Über die politische Verführbarkeit bürgerlichen Geistes* (1939, 1959), in *Gesammelte Schriften,* vol. 6 (Frankfurt, 1982), pp. 7–223.

10. M. Heidegger, *Sein und Zeit* (Halle, 1927), pp. 235ff.

11. R. Descartes, *Meditationes de prima philosophia* (1641), in *Oeuvres de Descartes,* ed. Ch. Adam and P. Tannery, vol. 7 (repr. Paris, 1957), pp. 17ff.

12. Cf. especially K. O. Apel, *Transformation der Philosophie,* vol. 2 (Frankfurt, 1976), p. 221: "Cartesian radicalization of the transcendental point of view"; but above all pp. 392–93: "the methodical approach of Augustinian/Cartesian doubt . . . is obligatory . . . for ethics as well," because "the validity of moral norms (that is, the validity of the deontological claims of practical propositions) must, in principle, be bracketed and placed in question just as much as the truth-validity of theoretical propositions about facts."

13. R. Descartes, *Discours de la méthode* (1637), in *Oeuvres de Descartes,* ed. Ch. Adam and P. Tannery, vol. 6 (repr., Paris, 1956), pp. 22ff.: "morale par provision."

14. Cf. O. Marquard, 'Über die Unvermeidlichkeit von Üblichkeiten," in W. Oelmüller, ed., *Normen und Geschichte,* Materialien zur Normendiskussion 3 (Paderborn, 1979), pp. 332–42.

15. Cf. M. Kriele, *Theorie der Rechtsgewinnung* (Berlin, 1967), and also O. Marquard, *Farewell to Matters of Principle,* trans. Robert M. Wallace (Oxford, 1988) (= *Abschied vom Prinzipiellen* [Stuttgart, 1981]).

16. Cf. D. Böhler, discussion contribution, in K. O. Apel, D. Böhler, and G. Kadelbach, eds., *Praktische Philosophie/Ethik. Dialoge,* vol. 1 (Frankfurt, 1984), p. 159.

17. Cf. Hannah Arendt, *Eichmann in Jerusalem: A Report on the Banality of Evil* (New York, 1963).

18. Cf. O. Marquard, "Hegel un das Sollen," *Philosophisches Jahrbuch* 72 (1964): 103–19; reprinted in O. Marquard, *Schwierigkeiten mit der der Geschichtsphilosophie,* 2nd ed. (Frankfurt, 1982), pp. 37ff.

19. Cf. H. Schepers, "Zum Problem der Kotingenz bei Leibniz. Die beste der möglichen Welten," *Collegium Philosophicum. Studien, Joachim Ritter zum 60. Geburtstag,* ed. H. Lübbe et al. (Basel and Stuttgart, 1965), pp. 326–50.

20. The distinction that follows is inspired by S. Kierkegaard, *The Sickness unto Death* (1849), trans. W. Lowrie (Princeton, 1941), pp. 54ff.: the despair of possibility that is due to the lack of necessity, and the despair of necessity that is due to the lack of possibility.

21. Cf. W. Schapp, *In Geschichten verstrickt. Zum Sein von Mensch und Ding* (Hamburg, 1953). But especially see H. Lübbe, *Geschichtsbergriff und Ge-*

schichtsinteresse. Analytik und Pragmatik der Historie (Basel and Stuttgart, 1977). Cf. also R. Koselleck, "Der Zufall als Motivationsrest in der Geschichts-schreibung," in H. R. Jauss, ed., *Die nicht mehr schönen Künste,* Poetik und Hermeneutik 3 (Munich, 1968), pp. 129–41. Koselleck (p. 129) cities R. Aron, *Introduction à la philosophie de l'histoire.* (Paris, 1948), p. 20: "le hasard est le fondement de l'histoire."

22. Cf. E. Boutroux, *De la Contingence des lois de la nature* (1874), translated by F. Rothwell as *The Contingency of the Laws of Nature* (Chicago, 1916).

23. A. Malraux, *Anti-Memoirs,* trans. T. Kilmartin (New York, 1968), p. 1.

24. For Montesquieu I follow *Oeuvres complètes,* ed. R. Caillois, vol. 2 (Paris, 1958), pp. 396ff.

25. Cf. F. Schalk, ed., *Die französischen Moralisten,* vol. 1 (Munich, 1973), pp. 203–57. Cf. the editor's introduction, esp. pp. 32ff.

26. Cf. M. Hossenfelder, introduction to Sextus Empiricus, *Grundriss der pyrrho-nischen Skepsis* (Frankfurt, 1968), esp. pp. 42ff.

27. This thesis about freedom—a thesis that is only suggested here, and by no means adequately worked out—is an attempt to cross and to blend the idea of freedom that comes from the political doctrine of the separation of powers with the idea of freedom that comes from the philosophical doctrine of levels. Cf. N. Hartmann, *Ethik* (1925) (3rd printing, Berlin, 1949), pp. 621–821, esp. pp. 649–50: "The causal nexus and the surplus of determination." Cf. also N. Hartmann, *Der Aufbau der realen Welt* (1939) (3rd printing, Berlin, 1964), pp. 493ff. and 510ff., esp. p. 519: "A world in which there is freedom must have at least two levels. In a multileveled world, categorical freedom makes its appear-ance, between one level and the next, as a phenomenon accompanying the novelty in the higher type of determination. Then there are as many kinds of freedom as there are distances between levels. In a single-leveled world, with one type of determination only, freedom is an impossibility." The doctrine of freedom that goes with the theory of levels is hierarchical, while the doctrine of freedom that goes with the separation of powers is, precisely, nonhierarchical. The cross between the two that is attempted here results in a dehierarchizing of the solution from the theory of levels and in an ontological broadening of the solution from the theory of the separation of powers. The outcome, I hope, is a doctrine of freedom as plurality of determination.

28. J. Ritter, "Über das Lachen" (1940), in J. Ritter, *Subjektivität, Sechs Aufsätze* (Frankfurt, 1974), pp. 62–92. H. Plessner, "Lachen und Weinen. Ein Untersuch-ung der Grenzen menschlichen Verhaltens" (1941), in H. Plessner, *Gesammelte Schriften,* vol. 7 (Frankfurt, 1982), pp. 201–387. Cf. O. Marquard, "Vernunft als Grenzreaktion," in H. Poser, ed., *Wandel des Vernunftbegriffs* (Freiburg and Munich, 1981), pp. 107–33. See also O. Marquard, "Loriot lauréat. Laudatio auf Bernhard-Viktor von Bülow bei der Verleihung des Kasseler Literatur-

preises für grotesken Humor 1985," in *Wilhelm-Busch-Jahrbuch 1985,* Mitteil-ungen der Wilhelm-Busch-Gesellschaft, no. 51 (Hannover, 1986), pp. 81–85.

Translator's Notes

a. The "opposition" Marquard refers to is, of course, opposition to the Nazi regime.

b. On Hegel's critique of deontological thinking—his "Sollenskritik"—see trans-lator's note g to "On the Dietetics of the Expectation of Meaning" (chapter 3).

Note on the Selections

"Skeptics," a speech of thanks on receiving the 1984 Sigmund Freud Prize for Scholarly Writing of the Deutsche Akademie für Sprache und Dichtung (Darmstadt, October 12, 1984), was published in the Akademie's *Jahrbuch 1984* (Heidelberg: Lambert Schneider, 1985), pp. 122–25.

"Unburdenings," a Fellow's Lecture at the Wissenschaftskolleg zu Berlin (February 9, 1983), was published in P. Wapnewski, ed., *Wissenschaftskolleg—Institute for Advanced Study—zu Berlin. Jahrbuch 1982/83* (Berlin: Seidler, 1984), pp. 245–58.

"On the Dietetics of the Expectation of Meaning," a lecture in the Studium Generale of the University at Mainz (July 4, 1983), was published in G. B. Aschenbach, ed., *Philosophische Praxis,* Schriftenreihe zur Philosophischen Praxis, vol. 1 (Cologne: Dinter, 1984), pp. 145–60.

"Universal History and Multiversal History," a lecture in the Studium Generale of the University at Freiburg (April 28, 1982), was published in *Saeculum. Zeitschrift für Universalgeschichte* 33 (1982): 106–15.

"The Age of Unworldliness?" a lecture at the colloquium, "Arbeitsgesellschaft. Wandel ihrer Strukturen," of the Walter Raymond Foundation (March 12, 1984, in Munich), was published in *Arbeitsgesellschaft,* Veröffentlichungen der Walter-Raymond-Stiftung, vol. 23 (Cologne: Bachern, 1984), pp. 11–28, and in *Giessener Universitätsblätter* 2 (1985): 9–20.

"On the Unavoidability of the Human Sciences," the opening address of the annual meeting of the Westdeutsche Rektorenkonferenz (May 5, 1985), was published in Westdeutsche Rektorenkonferenz, ed., *Anspruch und Herausforderung. Jahresversammlung 1985* (Bonn: Dokumentationsabteilung der Westdeutschen Rektorenkonferenz 1985), pp. 47–67.

"In Defense of the Accidental," a lecture at the Salzburg Humanismusgespräch 1984 (September 20, 1984), was reworked in 1985–1986 and first published in the original, German edition of this volume.

All of these pieces appeared in that volume, *Apologie des Zufälligen. Philosophische Studien* (Stuttgart: Philipp Reklam, 1986), of which *In Defense of the Accidental* is a complete translation.

Name Index

Adler, A., 22
Anders, G., 60
Apel, K. O., 10, 68, 112, 114
Ariès, P., 20, 74
Aristotle, 39, 110–11
Augustine, 12, 112
Azaïs, 21, 27 *n*.18

Balzac, H., 21, 27 *n*.18
Bloch, E., 19
Blumenberg, H., 12, 16, 41, 72
Bohr, N., 91
Bopp, 93
Borst, A., 52
Boyle, R., 93
Buffon, 27 *n*.18, 55
Burckhardt, J., 22, 52, 56, 77, 93
Busch, W., 22, 29

Camus, A., 34, 45
Comte, A., 61, 72, 80
Condorcet, M., 72

Darwin, C., 55, 60–61, 72, 103, 111
Descartes, R., 14, 92, 112–15
Dilthey, W., 33, 60, 93, 103

Droysen, J. G., 16, 93
Dux, G., 61–62

Eichmann, A., 117
Emerson, R. W., 22
Epicurus, 11, 111

Feuchterslebeng, E. v., 38
Fichte, J. G., 9–10, 15, 18, 53, 72, 112
Formey, 27 *n*.18
Foucault, M., 55
Frankl, 33
Freud, S., 6, 33, 72

Galileo, 93
Gehlen, A., 10, 22–23, 60, 72
Goethe, vii
Grimm, 93

Habermas, J., 10, 18, 55, 68, 72, 112, 114
Hansen, 23
Harnack, A. V., 41
Hegel, G.W.F., 9, 16, 39, 42, 45, 53–54, 72, 109–10, 118
Heidegger, M., 32, 62, 73, 113
Heine, H., 9

Subject Index